1039501

GRAPHIC BIOGRAPHIES

ELEANOR ROOSEVELT
FIRST LADY OF THE WORLD

by Ryan Jacobson

illustrated by Gordon Purcell

and Barbara Schulz

Consultant:

F. Kennon Moody, PhD

Roosevelt Family Researcher

Lagrangeville, New York

Capstone press

Mankato, Minnesota

Graphic Library is published by Capstone Press,
151 Good Counsel Drive, P.O. Box 669, Mankato, Minnesota 56002.
www.capstonepress.com

Printed in the United States of America

1 2 3 4 5 6 10 09 08 07 06 05

Library of Congress Cataloging-in-Publication Data
Jacobson, Ryan.

Eleanor Roosevelt: First Lady of the world / by Ryan Jacobson; illustrated by Barbara Schulz and Gordon Purcell.

p. cm.—(Graphic library. Graphic biographies)

Summary: "Describes the life and work of U.S. First Lady Eleanor Roosevelt"—Provided by publisher.

Includes bibliographical references and index.

ISBN 0-7368-4969-6 (hardcover)

1. Roosevelt, Eleanor, 1884–1962—Juvenile literature. 2. Presidents' spouses—United States—Biography—Juvenile literature. I. Schulz, Barbara, (Artist) ill. II. Purcell, Gordon, ill. III. Title. IV. Series.

E807.1.R48J34 2006
973.917'09—dc22 2004028556

Art and Editorial Direction
Jason Knudson and Blake A. Hoena
Designers
Jason Knudson and Katherine Opseth
Illustrators
Gordon Purcell and Barbara Schulz
Editor
Angie Kaelberer

Editor's note: Direct quotations from primary sources are indicated by a yellow background.

Direct quotations appear on the following pages:

Pages 7, 22, 23, 25, 26, from *The Autobiography of Eleanor Roosevelt,* by Eleanor Roosevelt (New York: Harper & Brothers, 1961).

Page 16, from *Eleanor Roosevelt: An American Conscience*, by Tamara K. Hareven (Chicago: Quadrangle Books, 1968).

Page 11, from Franklin and Eleanor Roosevelt Institute, http://www.feri.org.

Page 18, from Penn Library Exhibitions: Marian Anderson: A Life in Song, http://www.library.upenn.edu/exhibits/rbm/anderson/linimage.html.

Page 21, from *Eleanor and Franklin: The Story of Their Relationship, Based on Eleanor Roosevelt's Private Papers*, by Joseph P. Lash (New York: Norton, 1971).

Page 27 (top), from the Eleanor Roosevelt Memorials, Franklin D. Roosevelt Library, Hyde Park, New York.

Page 27 (bottom), from the National Park Service, http://www.nps.gov.

Cover illustration shows Eleanor's trip in 1933 to investigate working conditions in the coal mines of West Virginia.

Table of Contents

Chapter 1
Little Nell

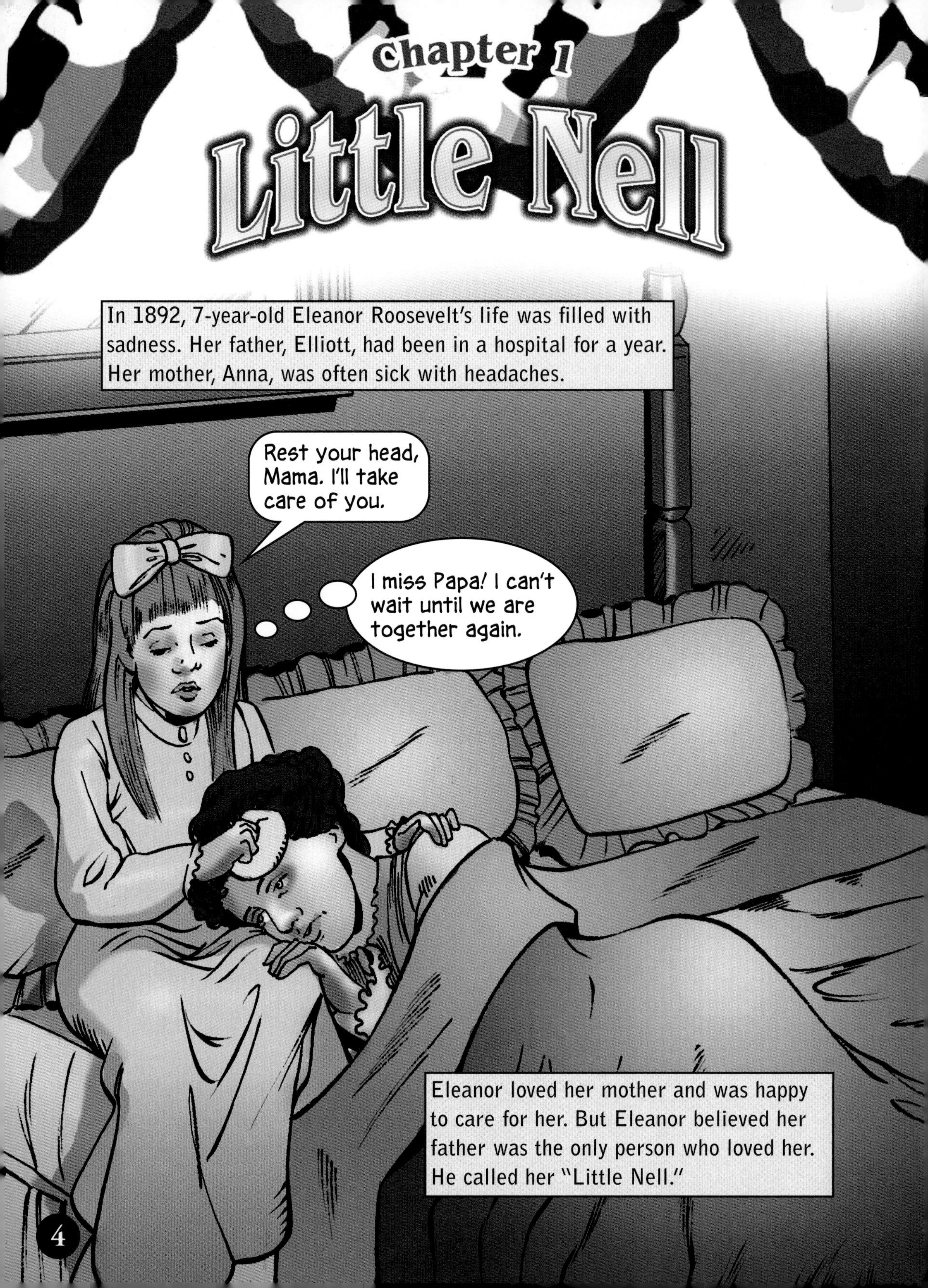
In 1892, 7-year-old Eleanor Roosevelt's life was filled with sadness. Her father, Elliott, had been in a hospital for a year. Her mother, Anna, was often sick with headaches.
Rest your head, Mama. I'll take care of you.
I miss Papa! I can't wait until we are together again.
Eleanor loved her mother and was happy to care for her. But Eleanor believed her father was the only person who loved her. He called her "Little Nell."

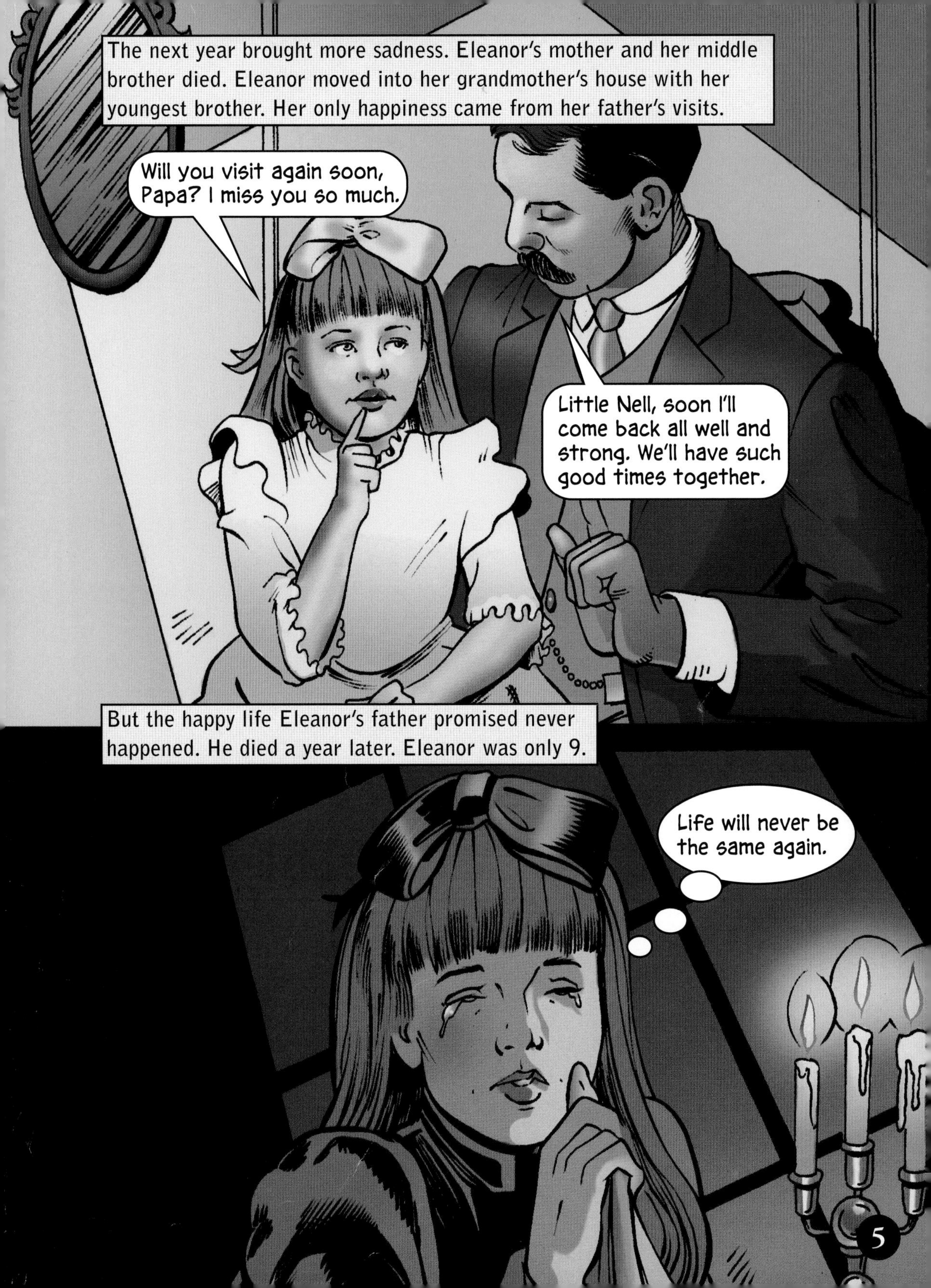
The next year brought more sadness. Eleanor's mother and her middle brother died. Eleanor moved into her grandmother's house with her youngest brother. Her only happiness came from her father's visits.
Will you visit again soon, Papa? I miss you so much.
Little Nell, soon I'll come back all well and strong. We'll have such good times together.
But the happy life Eleanor's father promised never happened. He died a year later. Eleanor was only 9.
Life will never be the same again.

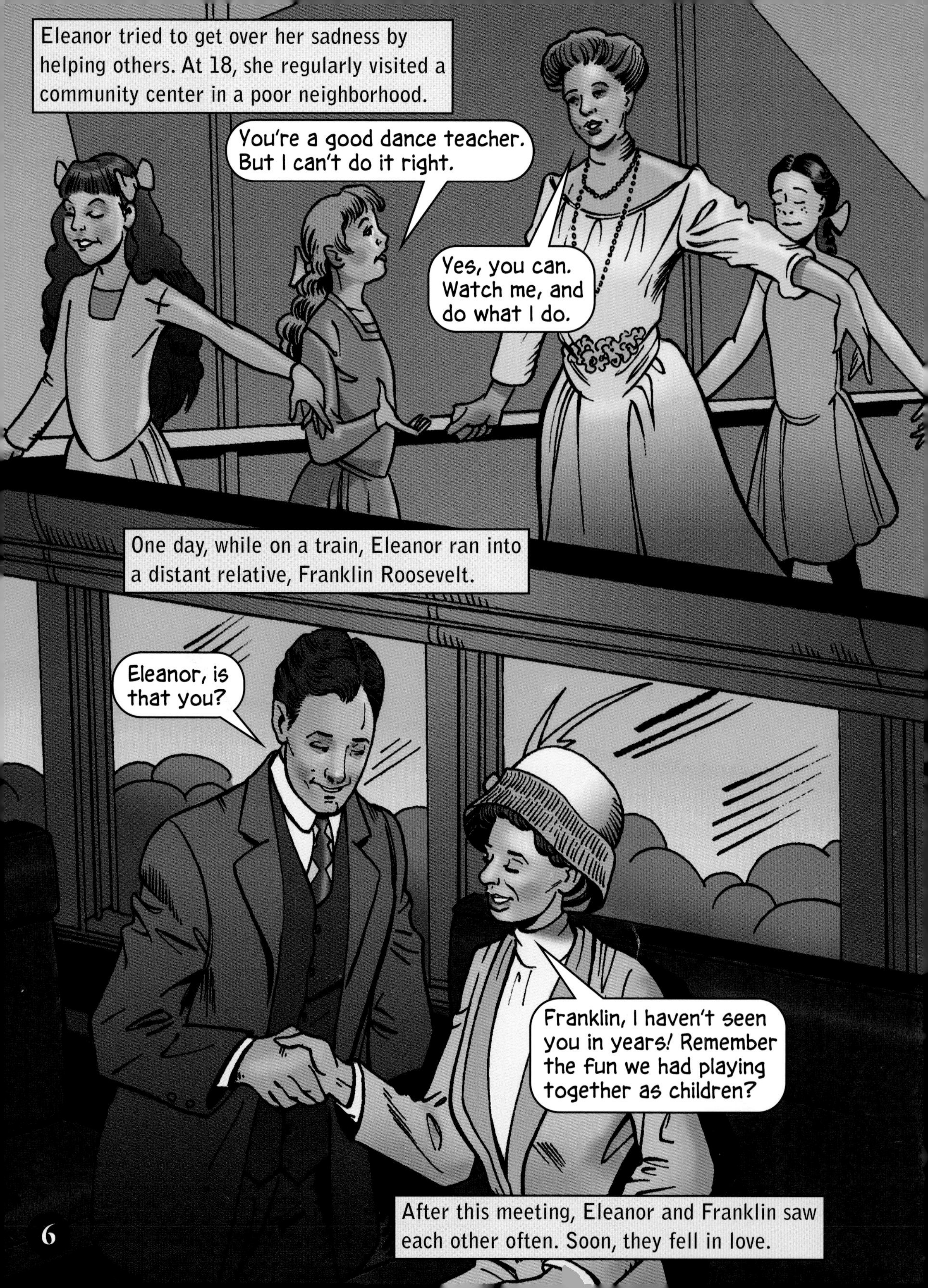
Eleanor tried to get over her sadness by helping others. At 18, she regularly visited a community center in a poor neighborhood.
You're a good dance teacher. But I can't do it right.
Yes, you can. Watch me, and do what I do.
One day, while on a train, Eleanor ran into a distant relative, Franklin Roosevelt.
Eleanor, is that you?
Franklin, I haven't seen you in years! Remember the fun we had playing together as children?
After this meeting, Eleanor and Franklin saw each other often. Soon, they fell in love.

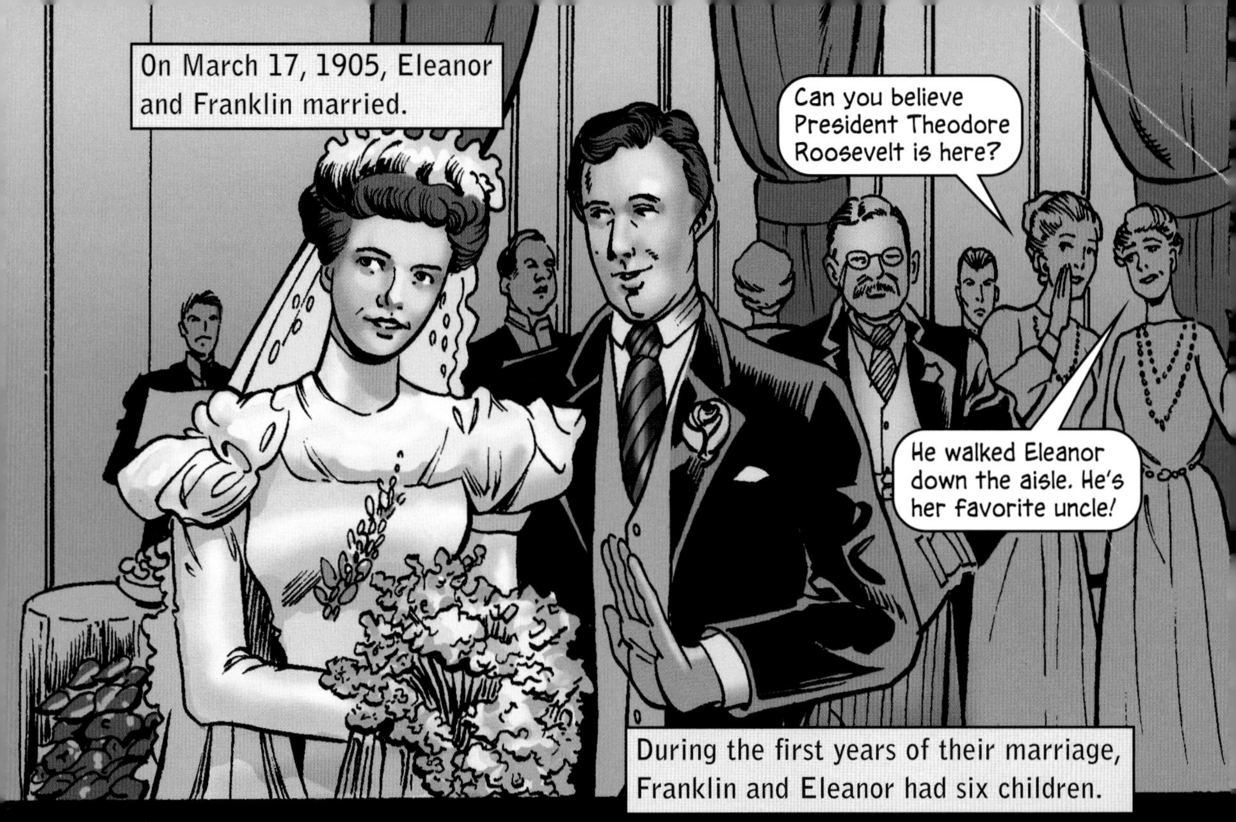
On March 17, 1905, Eleanor and Franklin married.
Can you believe President Theodore Roosevelt is here?
He walked Eleanor down the aisle. He's her favorite uncle!
During the first years of their marriage, Franklin and Eleanor had six children.

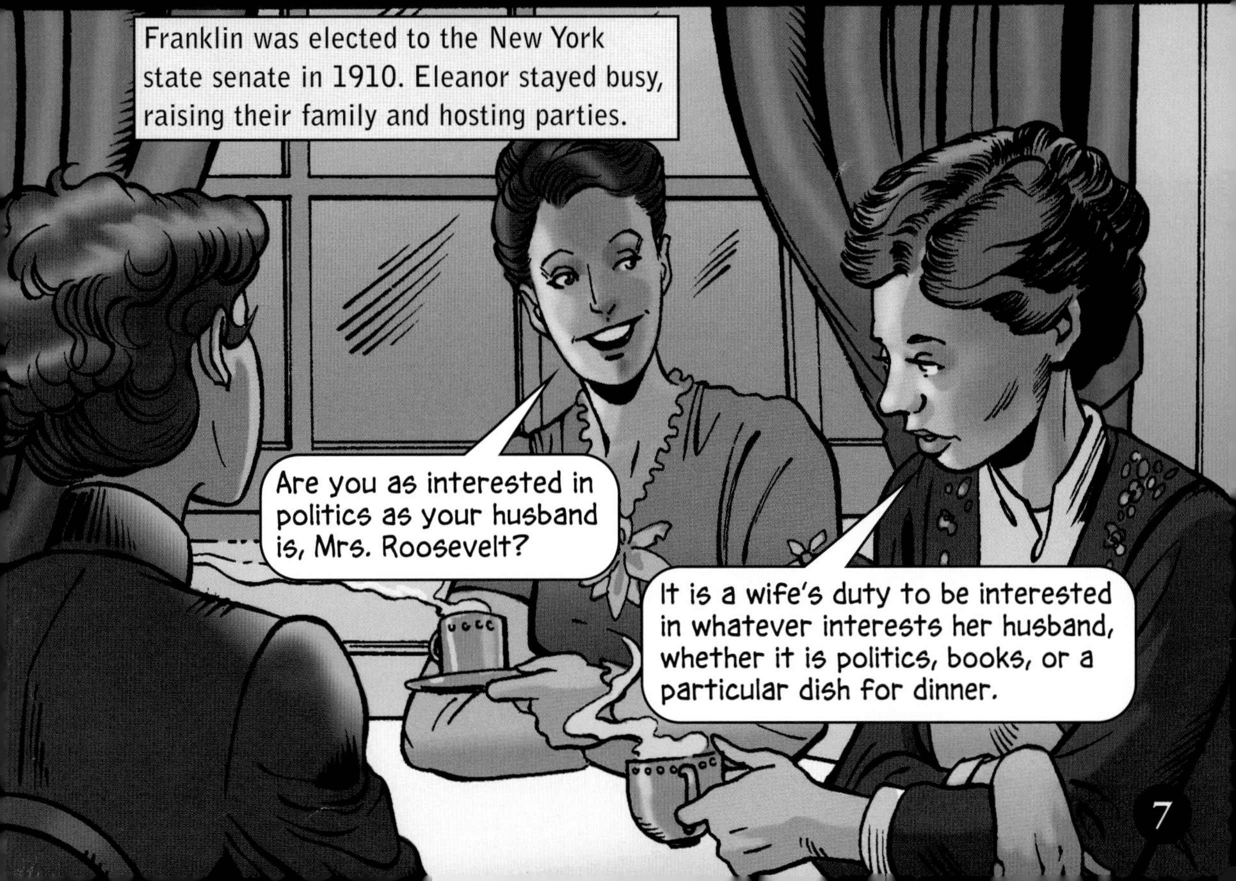
Franklin was elected to the New York state senate in 1910. Eleanor stayed busy, raising their family and hosting parties.
Are you as interested in politics as your husband is, Mrs. Roosevelt?
It is a wife's duty to be interested in whatever interests her husband, whether it is politics, books, or a particular dish for dinner.

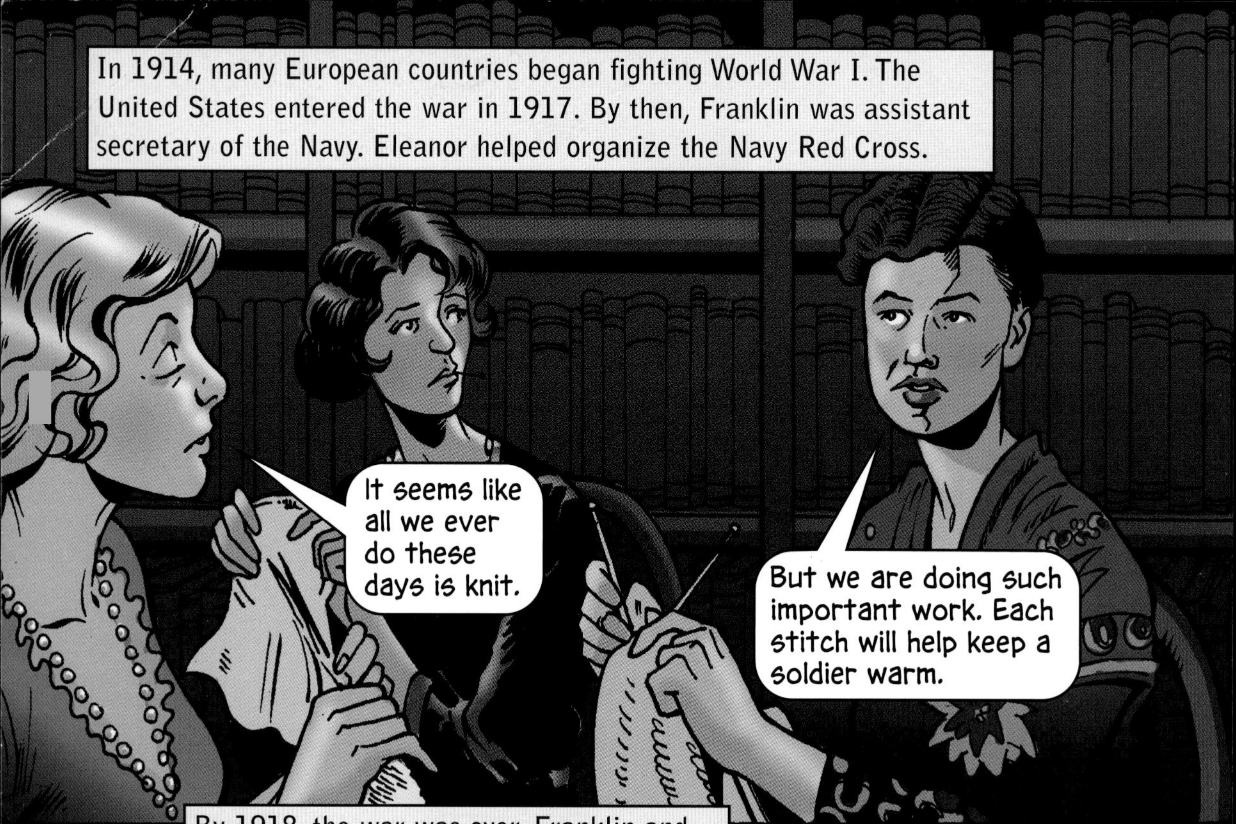
In 1914, many European countries began fighting World War I. The United States entered the war in 1917. By then, Franklin was assistant secretary of the Navy. Eleanor helped organize the Navy Red Cross.
It seems like all we ever do these days is knit.
But we are doing such important work. Each stitch will help keep a soldier warm.

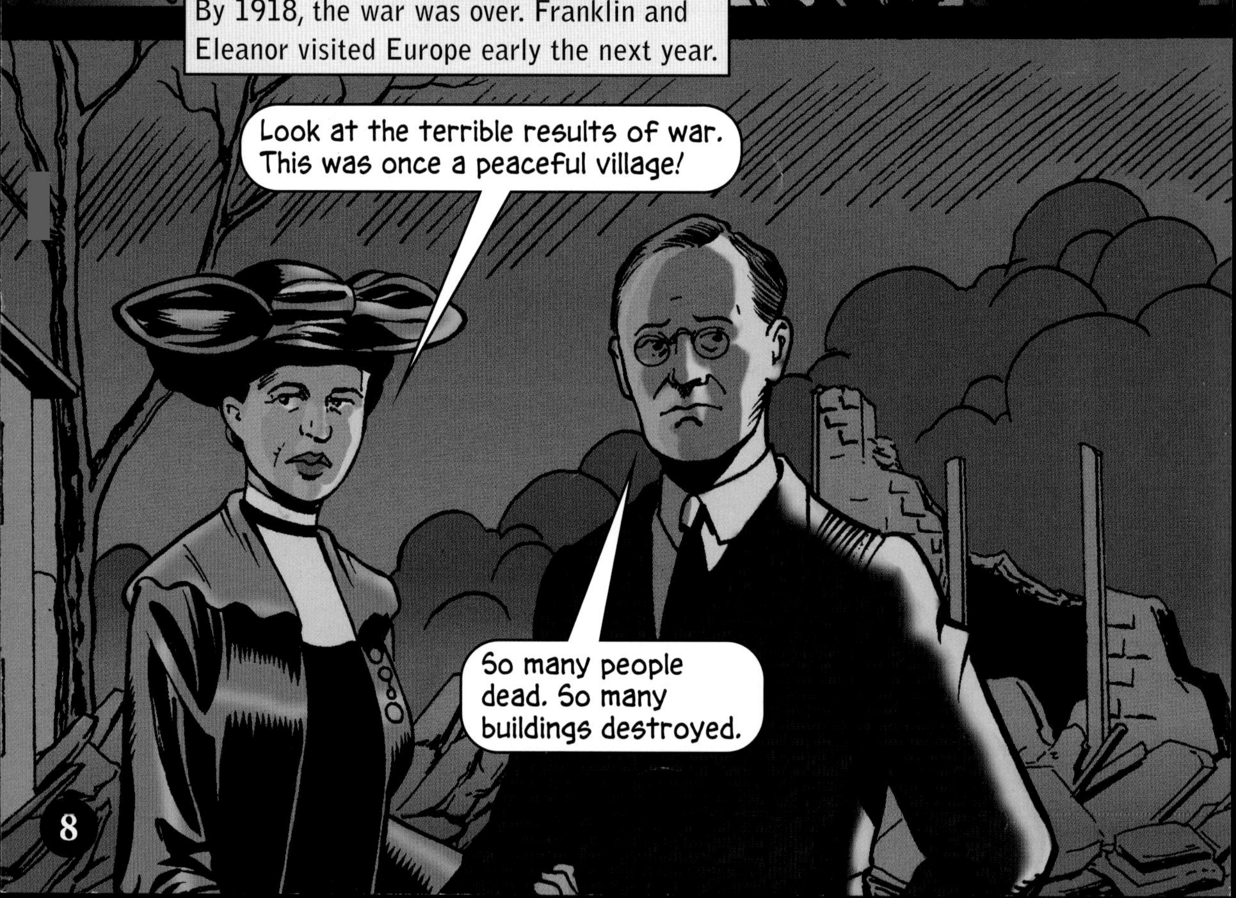
By 1918, the war was over. Franklin and Eleanor visited Europe early the next year.
Look at the terrible results of war. This was once a peaceful village!
So many people dead. So many buildings destroyed.

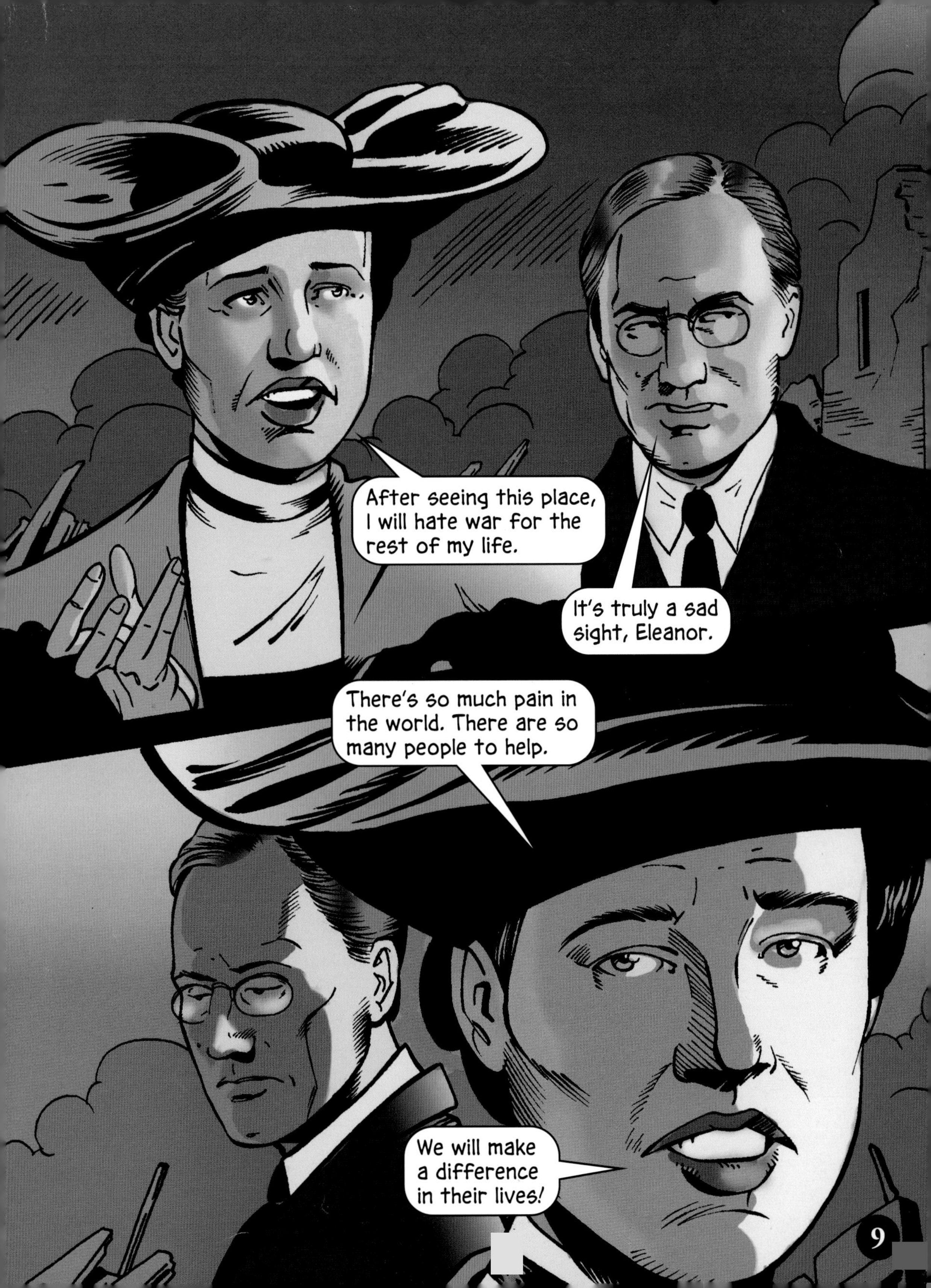
After seeing this place, I will hate war for the rest of my life.
It's truly a sad sight, Eleanor.
There's so much pain in the world. There are so many people to help.
We will make a difference in their lives!

Chapter 2
To the White House

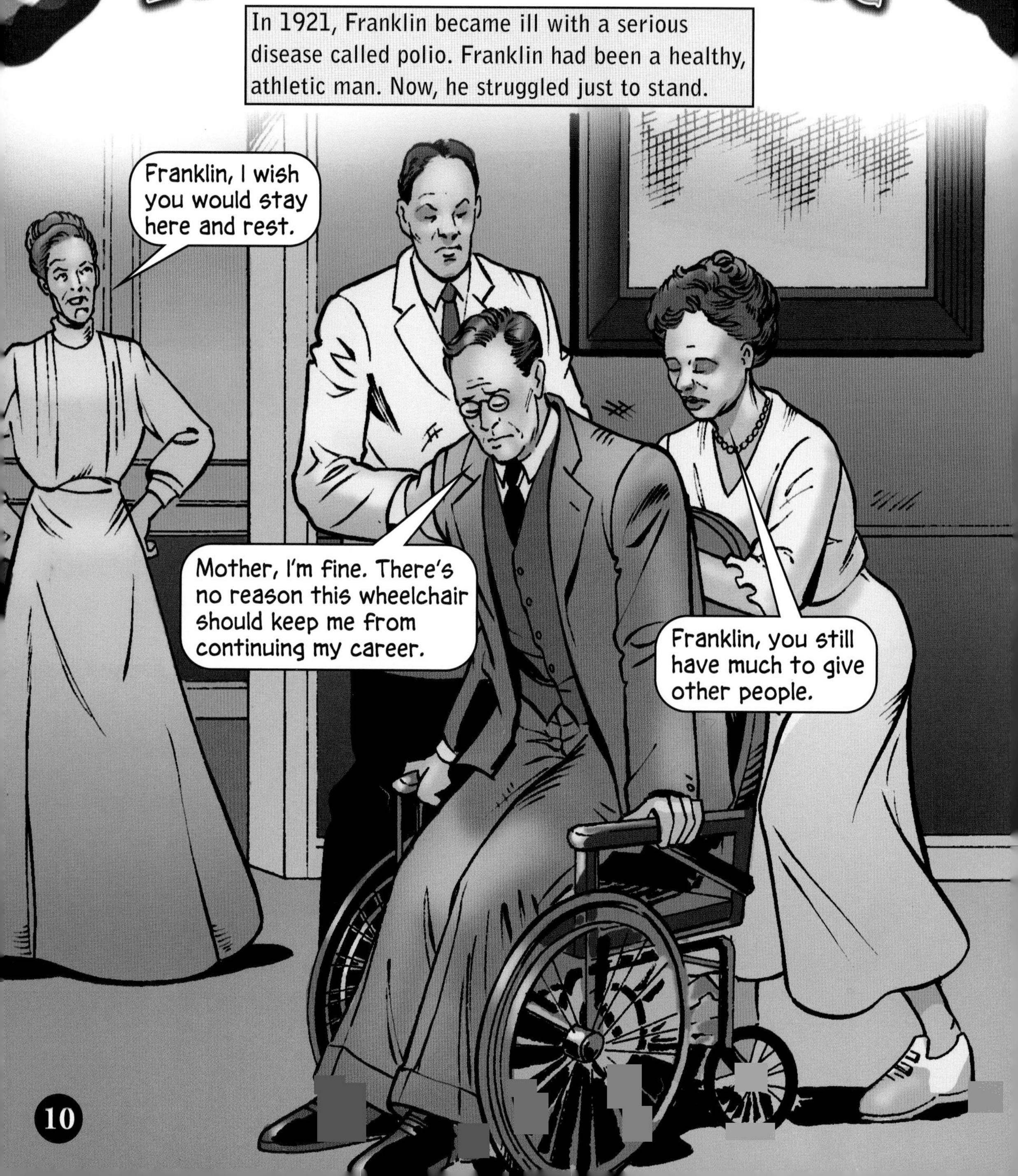
In 1921, Franklin became ill with a serious disease called polio. Franklin had been a healthy, athletic man. Now, he struggled just to stand.
Franklin, I wish you would stay here and rest.
Mother, I'm fine. There's no reason this wheelchair should keep me from continuing my career.
Franklin, you still have much to give other people.

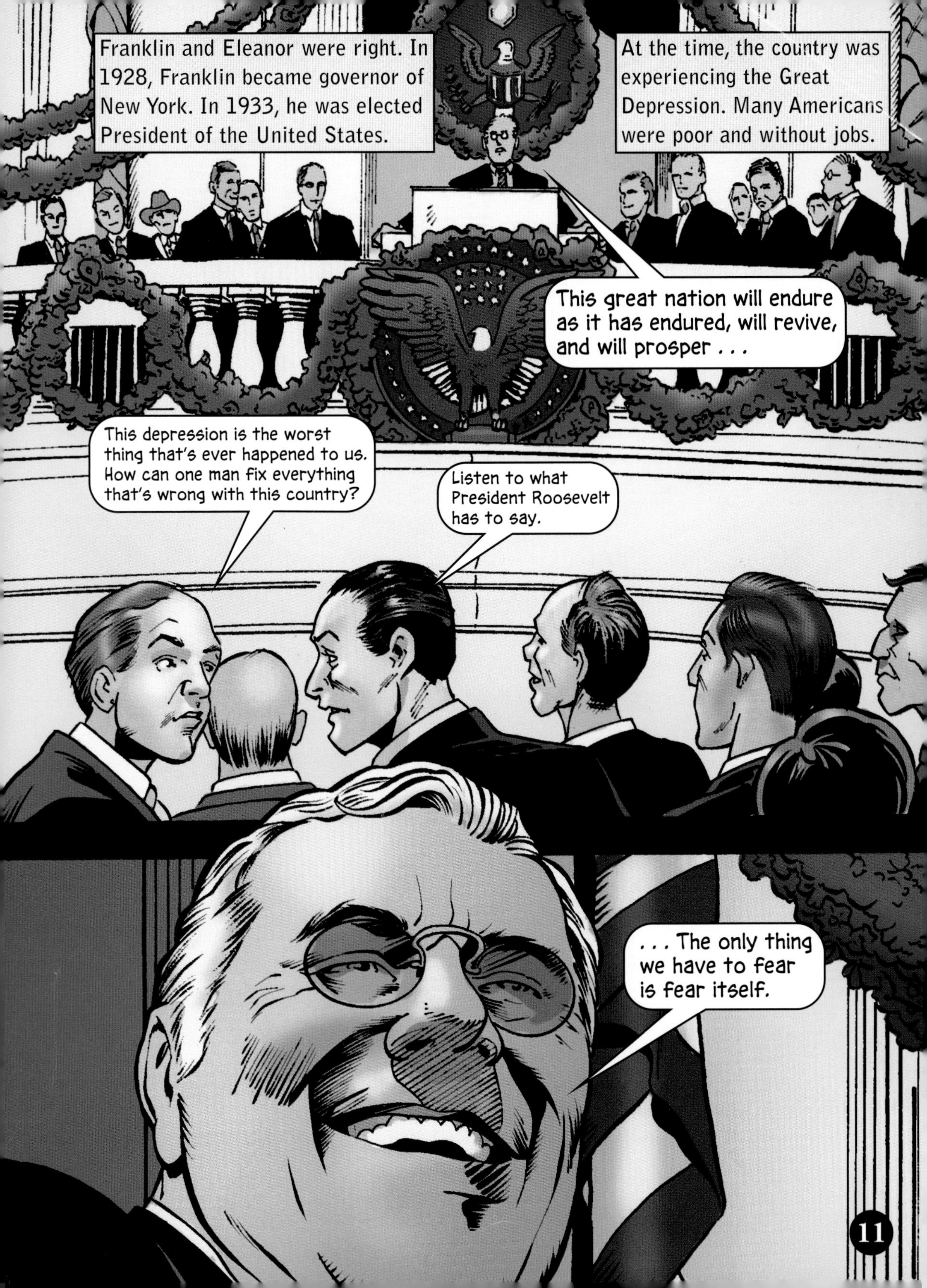
Franklin and Eleanor were right. In 1928, Franklin became governor of New York. In 1933, he was elected President of the United States.
At the time, the country was experiencing the Great Depression. Many Americans were poor and without jobs.
This great nation will endure as it has endured, will revive, and will prosper . . .
This depression is the worst thing that's ever happened to us. How can one man fix everything that's wrong with this country?
Listen to what President Roosevelt has to say.
. . . The only thing we have to fear is fear itself.

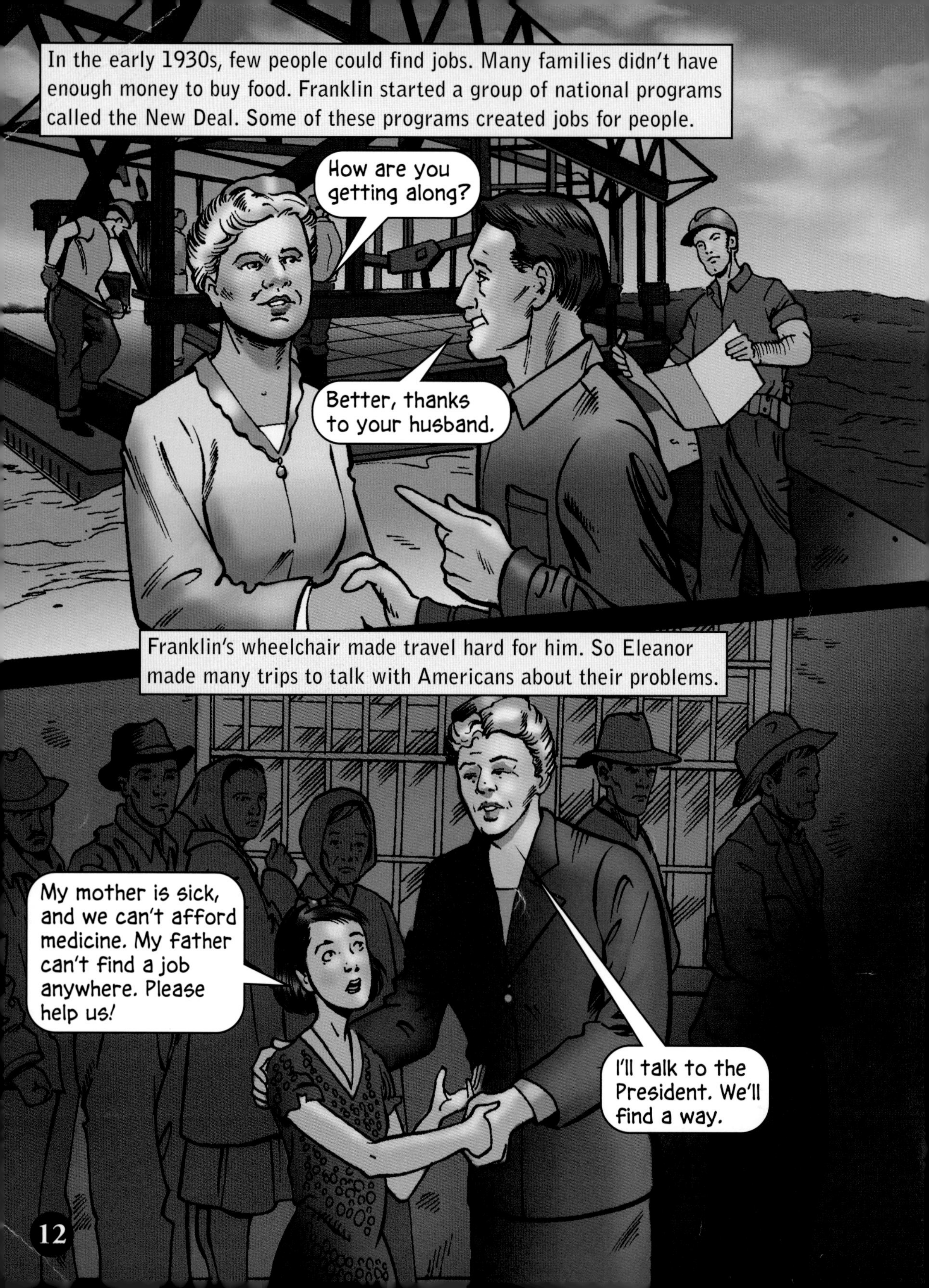
In the early 1930s, few people could find jobs. Many families didn't have enough money to buy food. Franklin started a group of national programs called the New Deal. Some of these programs created jobs for people.
How are you getting along?
Better, thanks to your husband.
Franklin's wheelchair made travel hard for him. So Eleanor made many trips to talk with Americans about their problems.
My mother is sick, and we can't afford medicine. My father can't find a job anywhere. Please help us!
I'll talk to the President. We'll find a way.

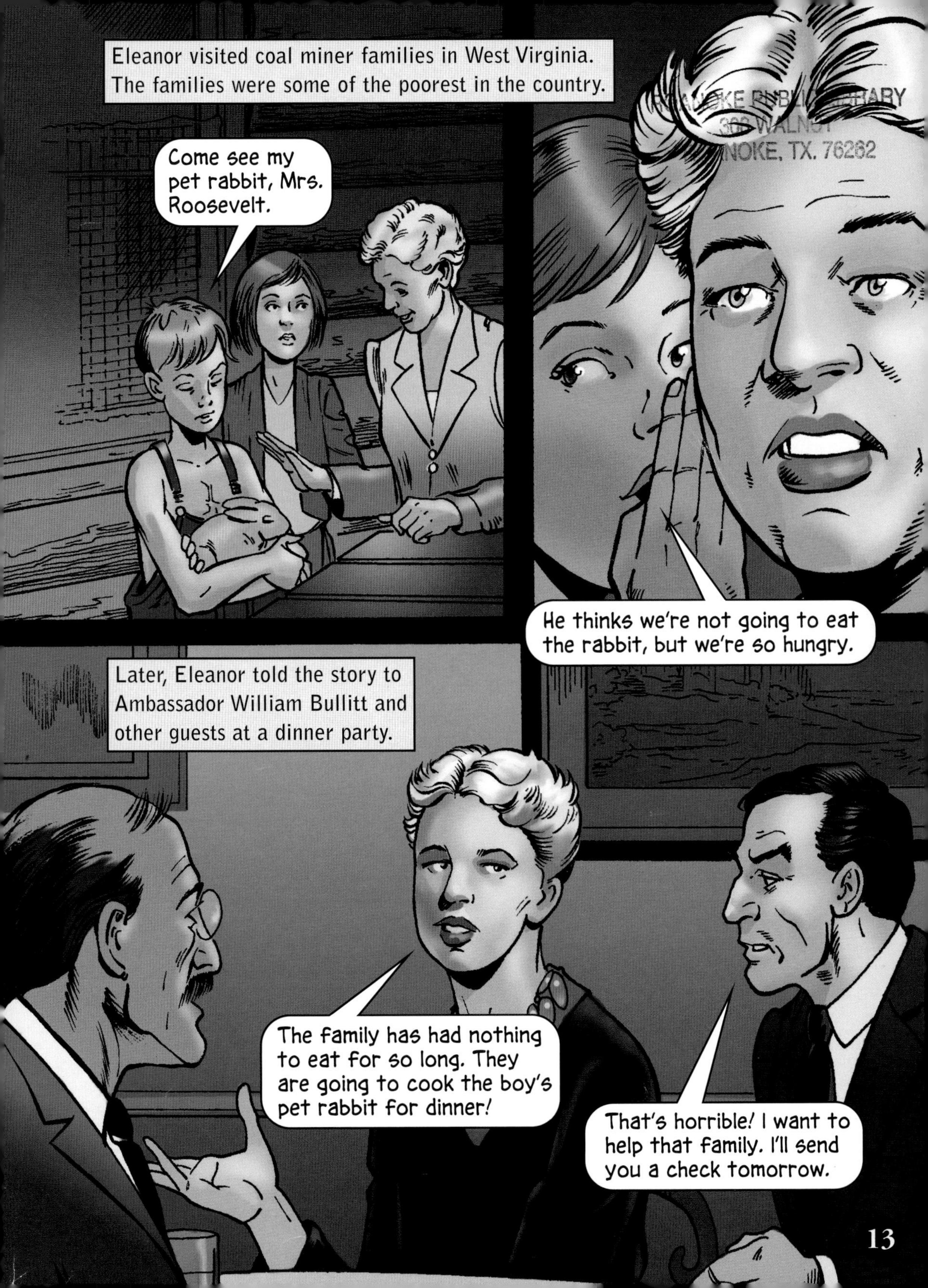
Eleanor visited coal miner families in West Virginia. The families were some of the poorest in the country.
Come see my pet rabbit, Mrs. Roosevelt.
He thinks we're not going to eat the rabbit, but we're so hungry.
Later, Eleanor told the story to Ambassador William Bullitt and other guests at a dinner party.
The family has had nothing to eat for so long. They are going to cook the boy's pet rabbit for dinner!
That's horrible! I want to help that family. I'll send you a check tomorrow.

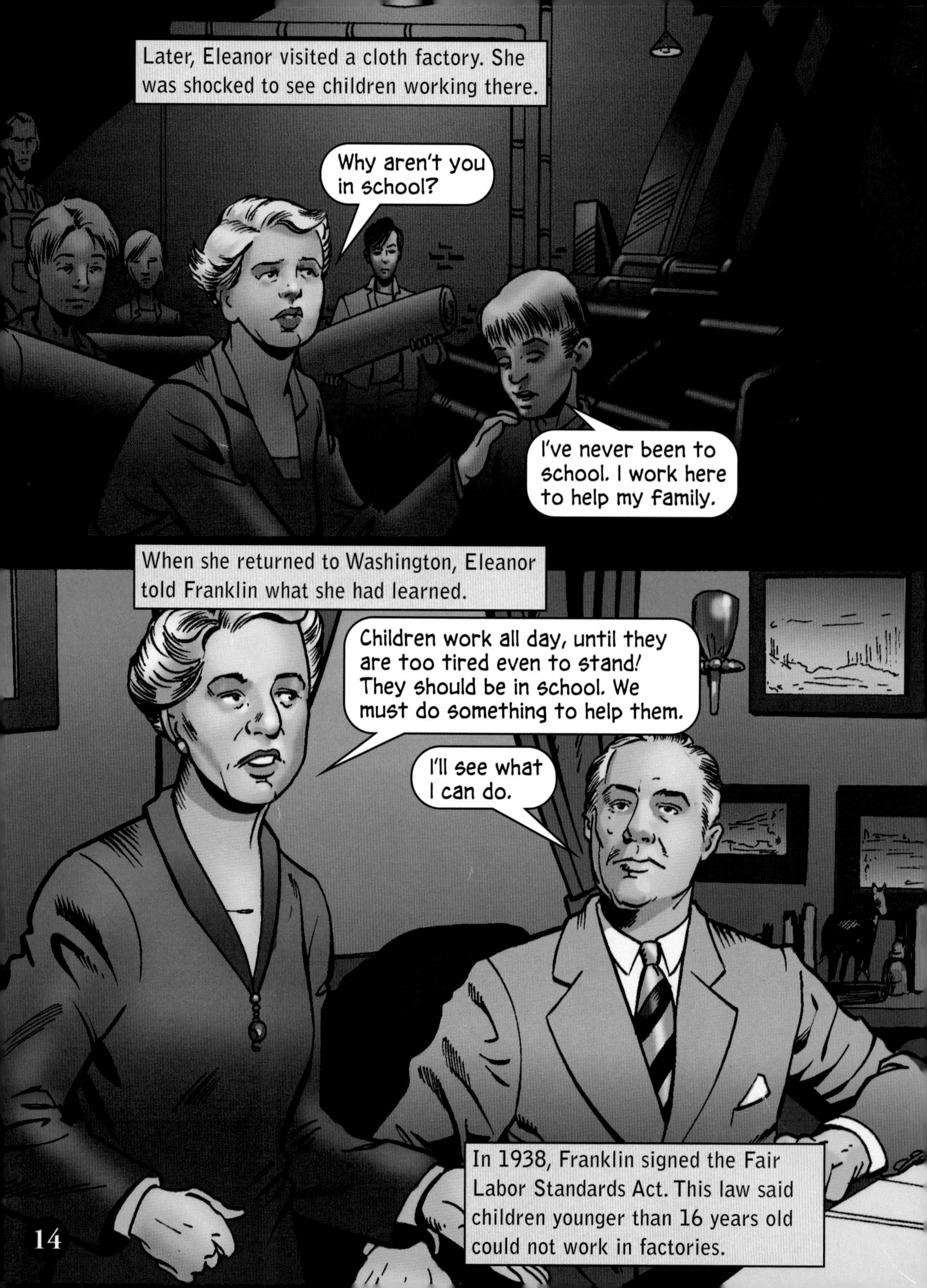
Later, Eleanor visited a cloth factory. She was shocked to see children working there.
Why aren't you in school?
I've never been to school. I work here to help my family.
When she returned to Washington, Eleanor told Franklin what she had learned.
Children work all day, until they are too tired even to stand! They should be in school. We must do something to help them.
I'll see what I can do.
In 1938, Franklin signed the Fair Labor Standards Act. This law said children younger than 16 years old could not work in factories.

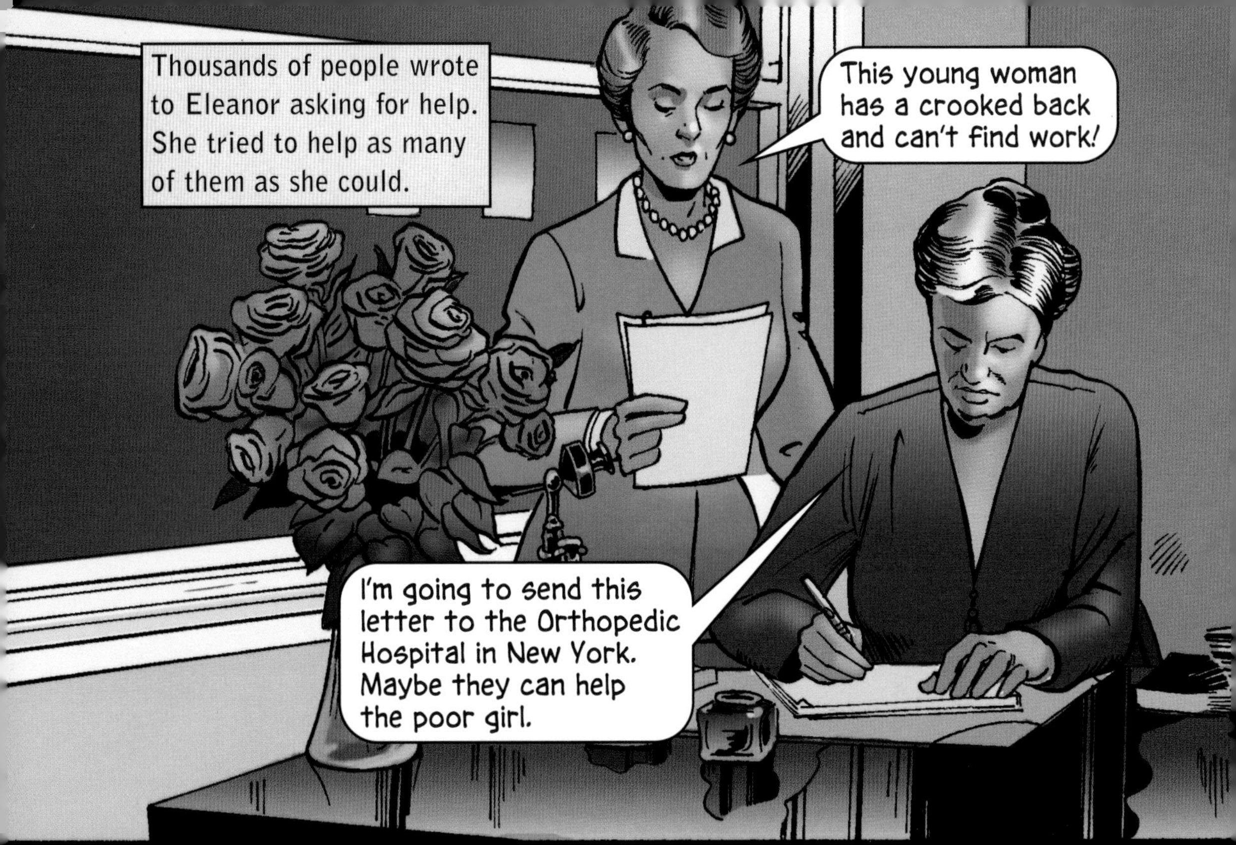
Thousands of people wrote to Eleanor asking for help. She tried to help as many of them as she could.
This young woman has a crooked back and can't find work!
I'm going to send this letter to the Orthopedic Hospital in New York. Maybe they can help the poor girl.

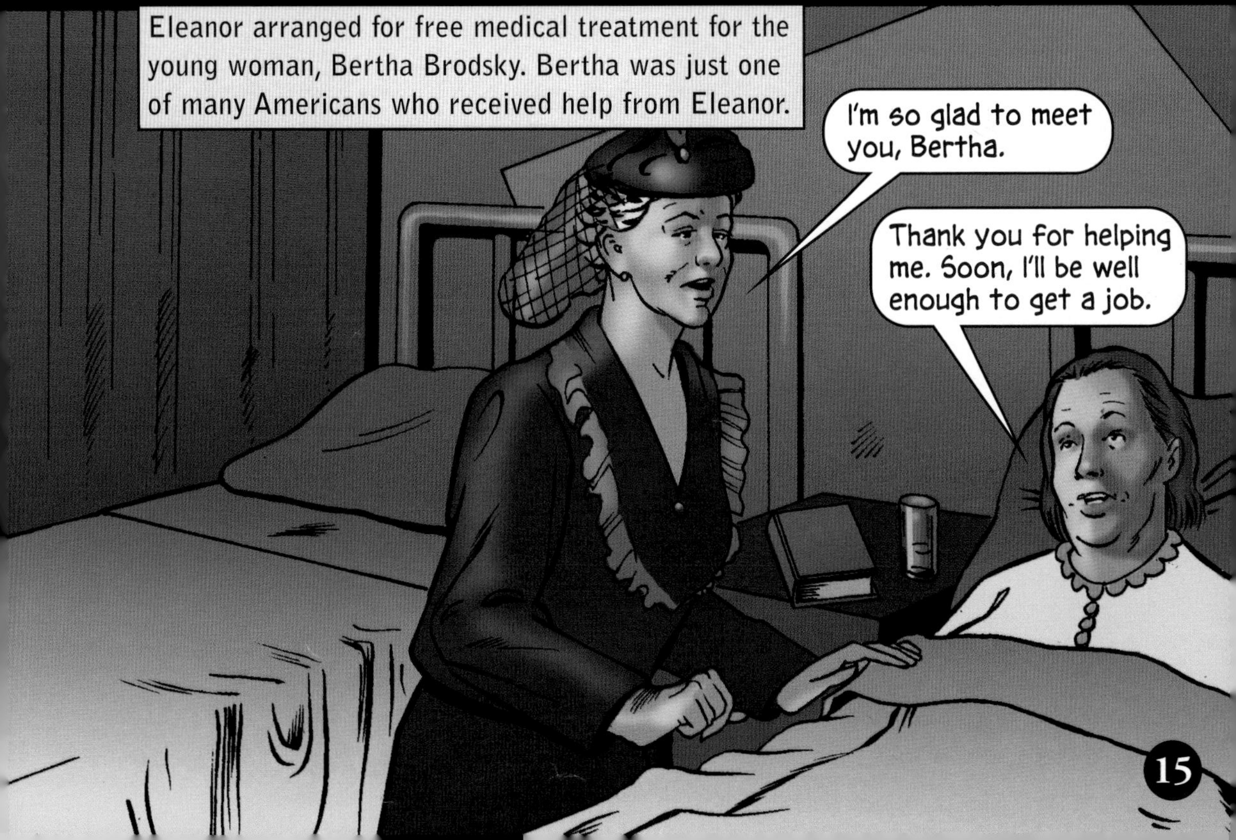
Eleanor arranged for free medical treatment for the young woman, Bertha Brodsky. Bertha was just one of many Americans who received help from Eleanor.
I'm so glad to meet you, Bertha.
Thank you for helping me. Soon, I'll be well enough to get a job.

Chapter 3
Eleanor to the Rescue

During the 1930s, women's problems received less attention than men's problems. Eleanor joined groups like the League of Women Voters and the Women's Trade Union League to help women gain more rights.

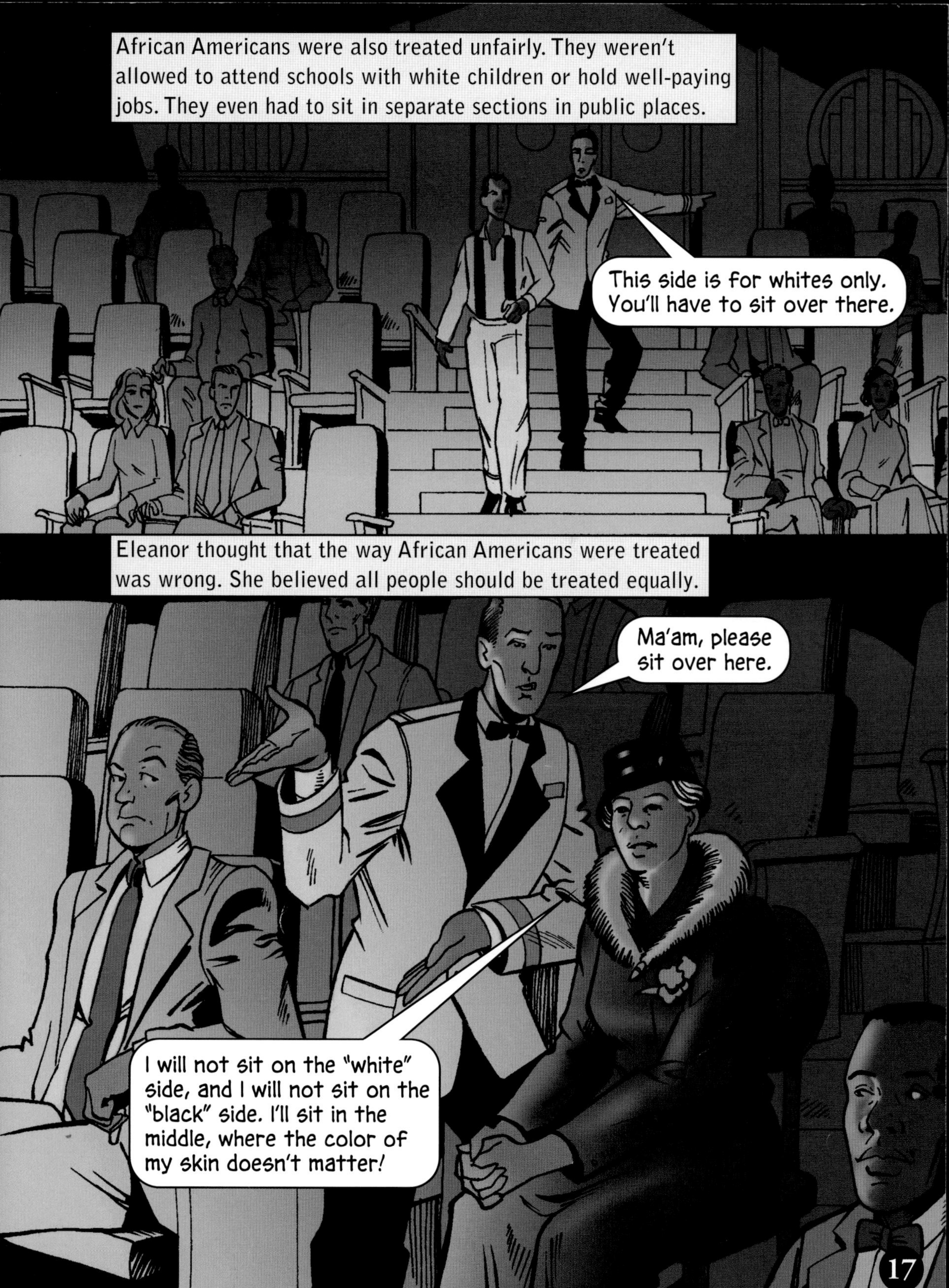
African Americans were also treated unfairly. They weren't allowed to attend schools with white children or hold well-paying jobs. They even had to sit in separate sections in public places.
This side is for whites only. You'll have to sit over there.
Eleanor thought that the way African Americans were treated was wrong. She believed all people should be treated equally.
Ma'am, please sit over here.
I will not sit on the "white" side, and I will not sit on the "black" side. I'll sit in the middle, where the color of my skin doesn't matter!

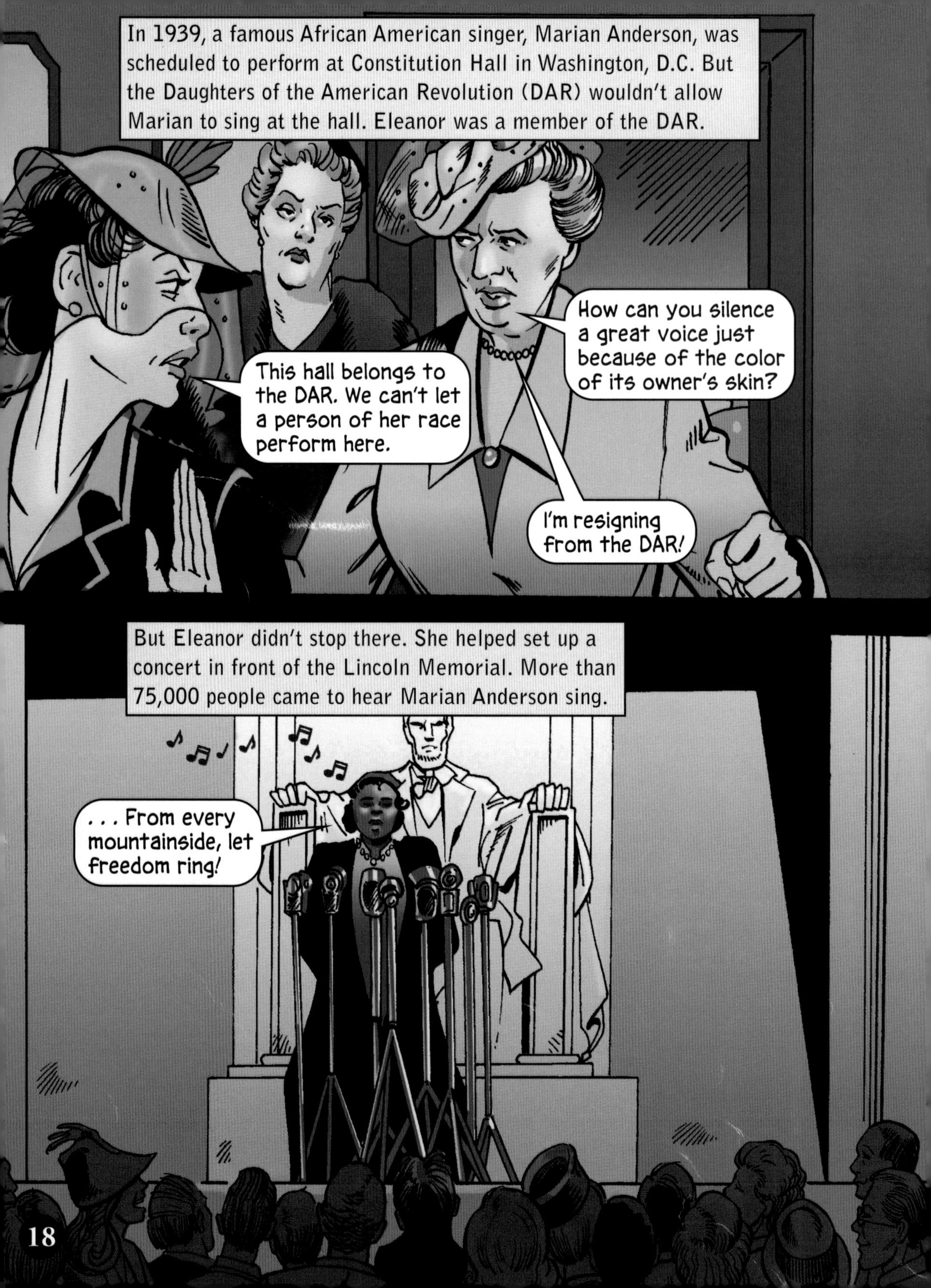
In 1939, a famous African American singer, Marian Anderson, was scheduled to perform at Constitution Hall in Washington, D.C. But the Daughters of the American Revolution (DAR) wouldn't allow Marian to sing at the hall. Eleanor was a member of the DAR.
This hall belongs to the DAR. We can't let a person of her race perform here.
How can you silence a great voice just because of the color of its owner's skin?
I'm resigning from the DAR!
But Eleanor didn't stop there. She helped set up a concert in front of the Lincoln Memorial. More than 75,000 people came to hear Marian Anderson sing.
. . . From every mountainside, let freedom ring!

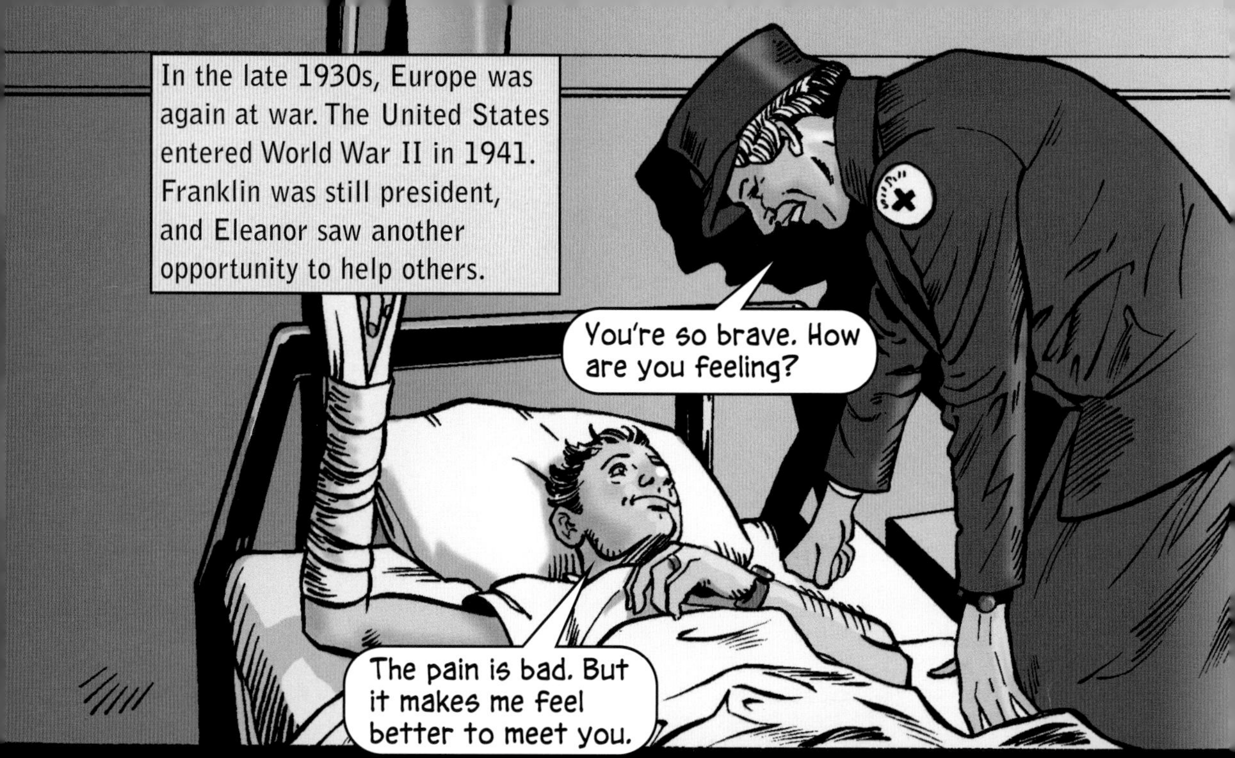
In the late 1930s, Europe was again at war. The United States entered World War II in 1941. Franklin was still president, and Eleanor saw another opportunity to help others.
You're so brave. How are you feeling?
The pain is bad. But it makes me feel better to meet you.

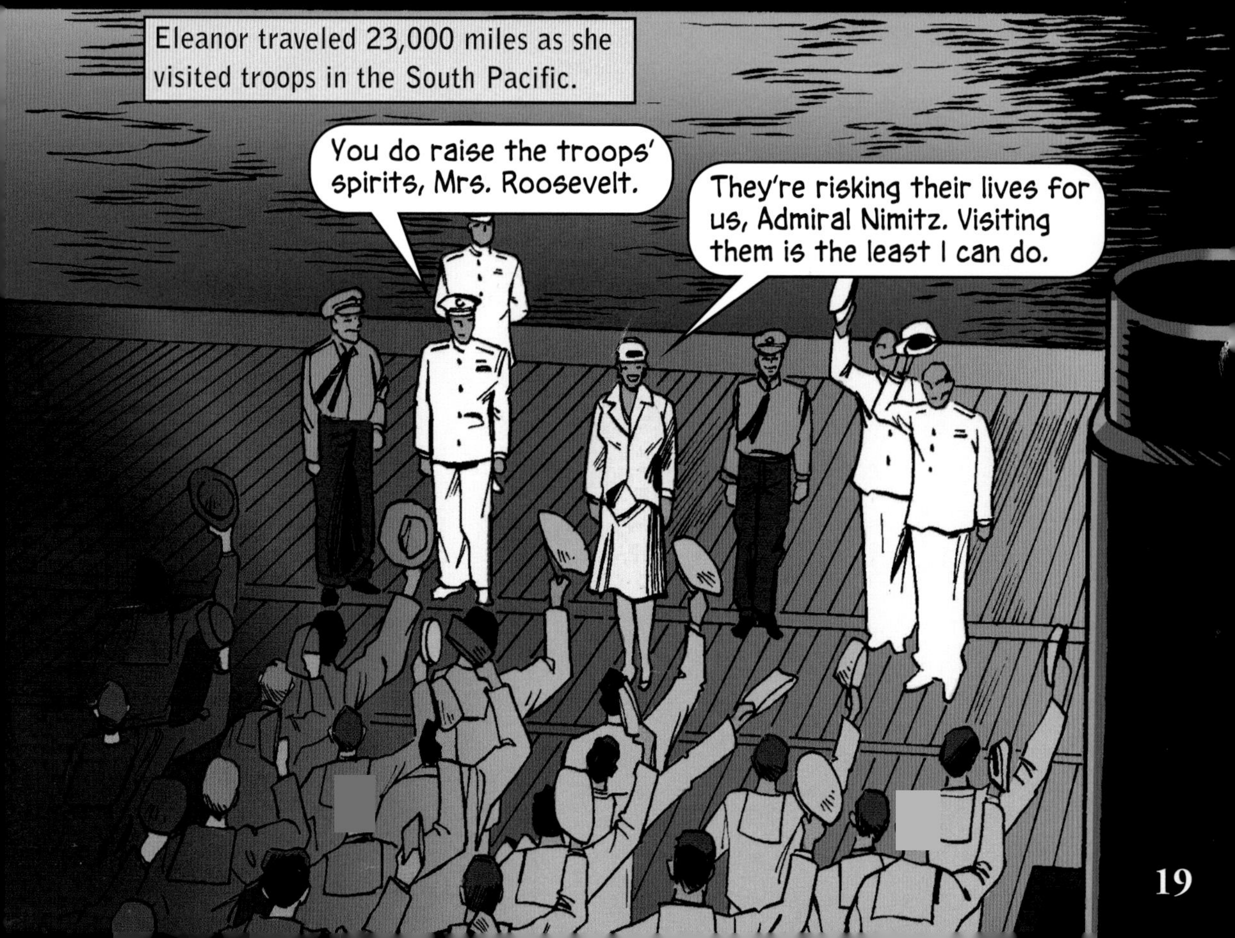
Eleanor traveled 23,000 miles as she visited troops in the South Pacific.
You do raise the troops' spirits, Mrs. Roosevelt.
They're risking their lives for us, Admiral Nimitz. Visiting them is the least I can do.

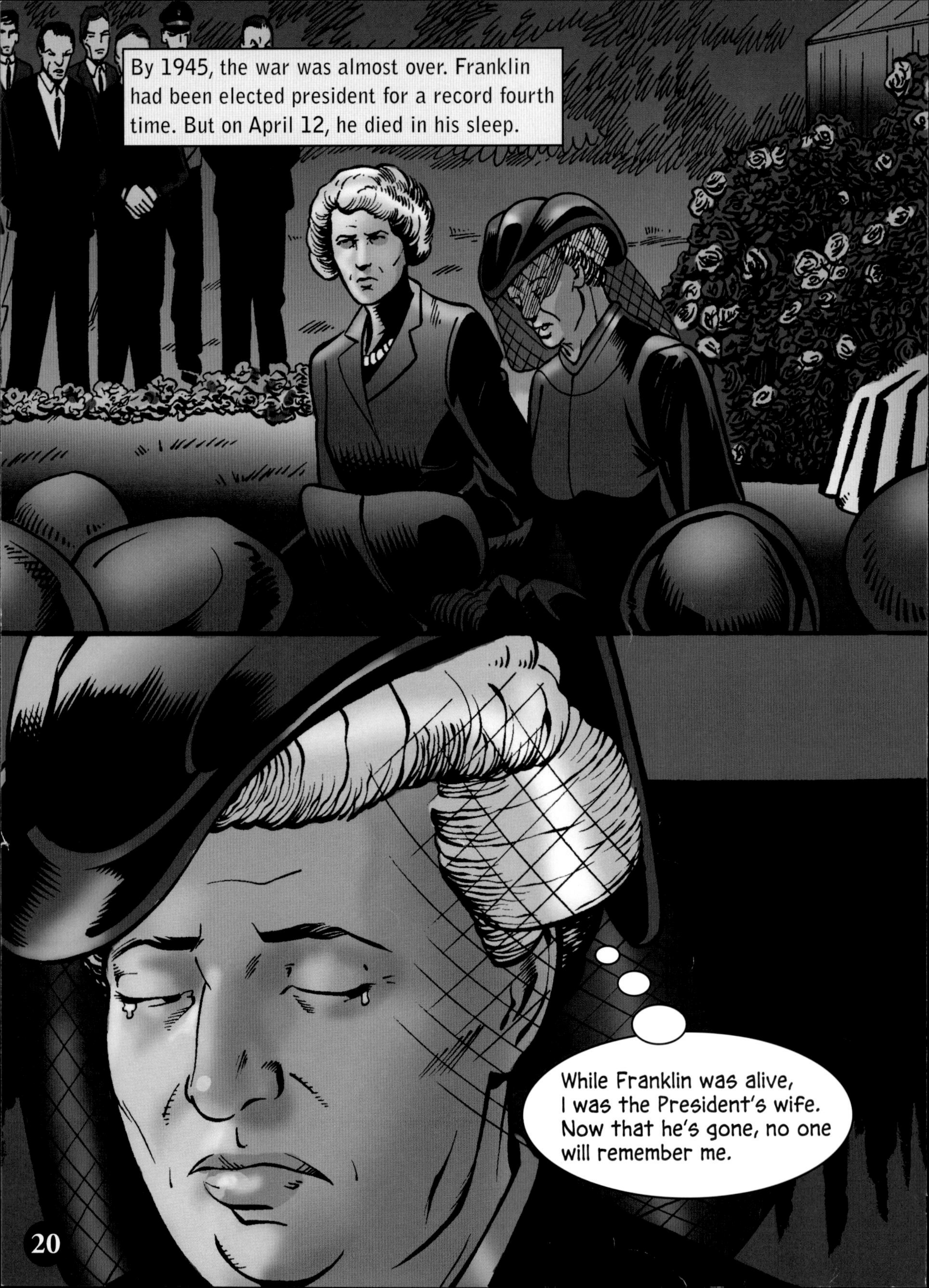
By 1945, the war was almost over. Franklin had been elected president for a record fourth time. But on April 12, he died in his sleep.
While Franklin was alive, I was the President's wife. Now that he's gone, no one will remember me.

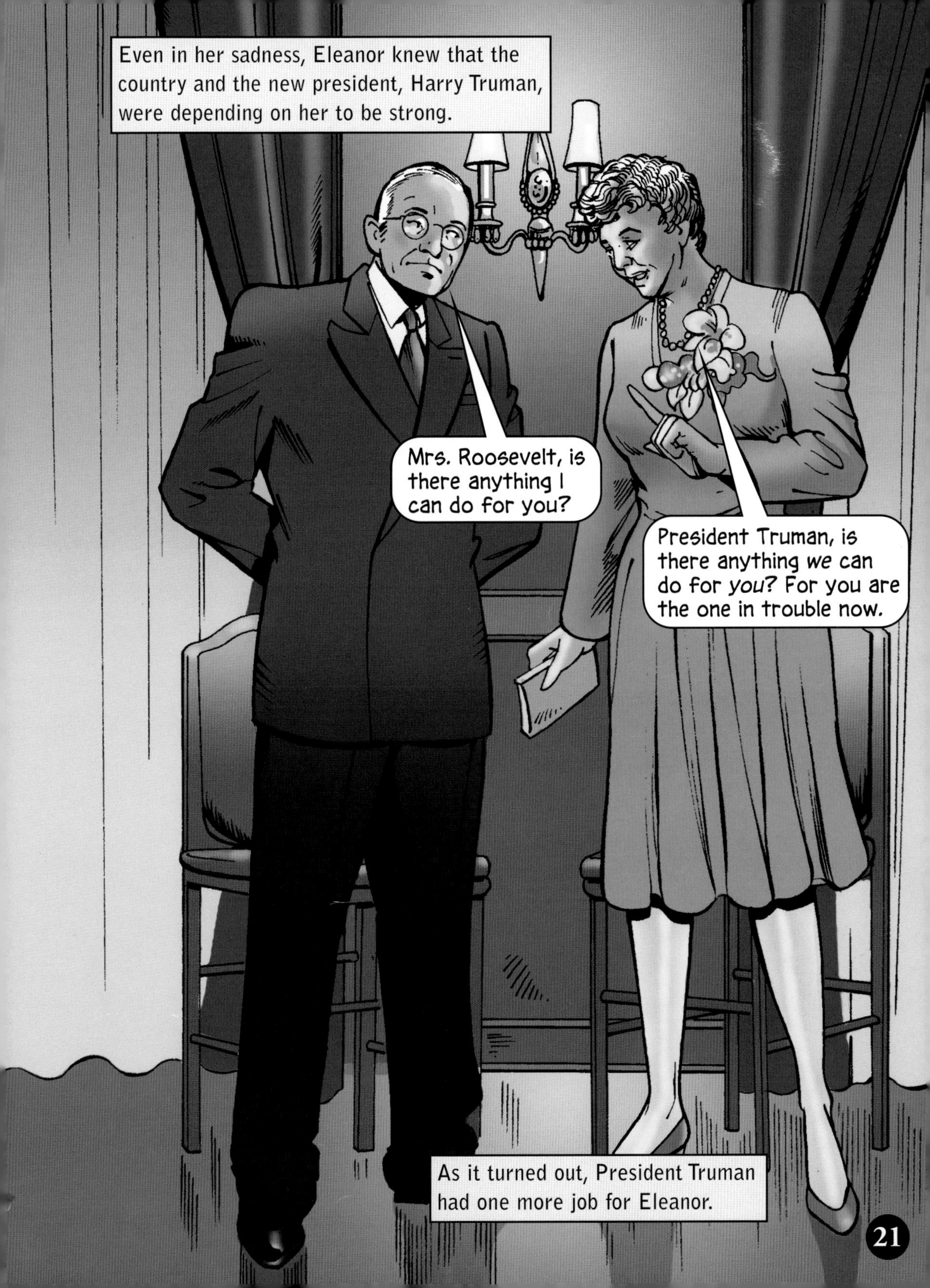
Even in her sadness, Eleanor knew that the country and the new president, Harry Truman, were depending on her to be strong.
Mrs. Roosevelt, is there anything I can do for you?
President Truman, is there anything *we* can do for *you*? For you are the one in trouble now.
As it turned out, President Truman had one more job for Eleanor.

Chapter 4

First Lady of the World

In October 1945, 50 countries formed an organization to work for world peace and human rights. It was called the United Nations.

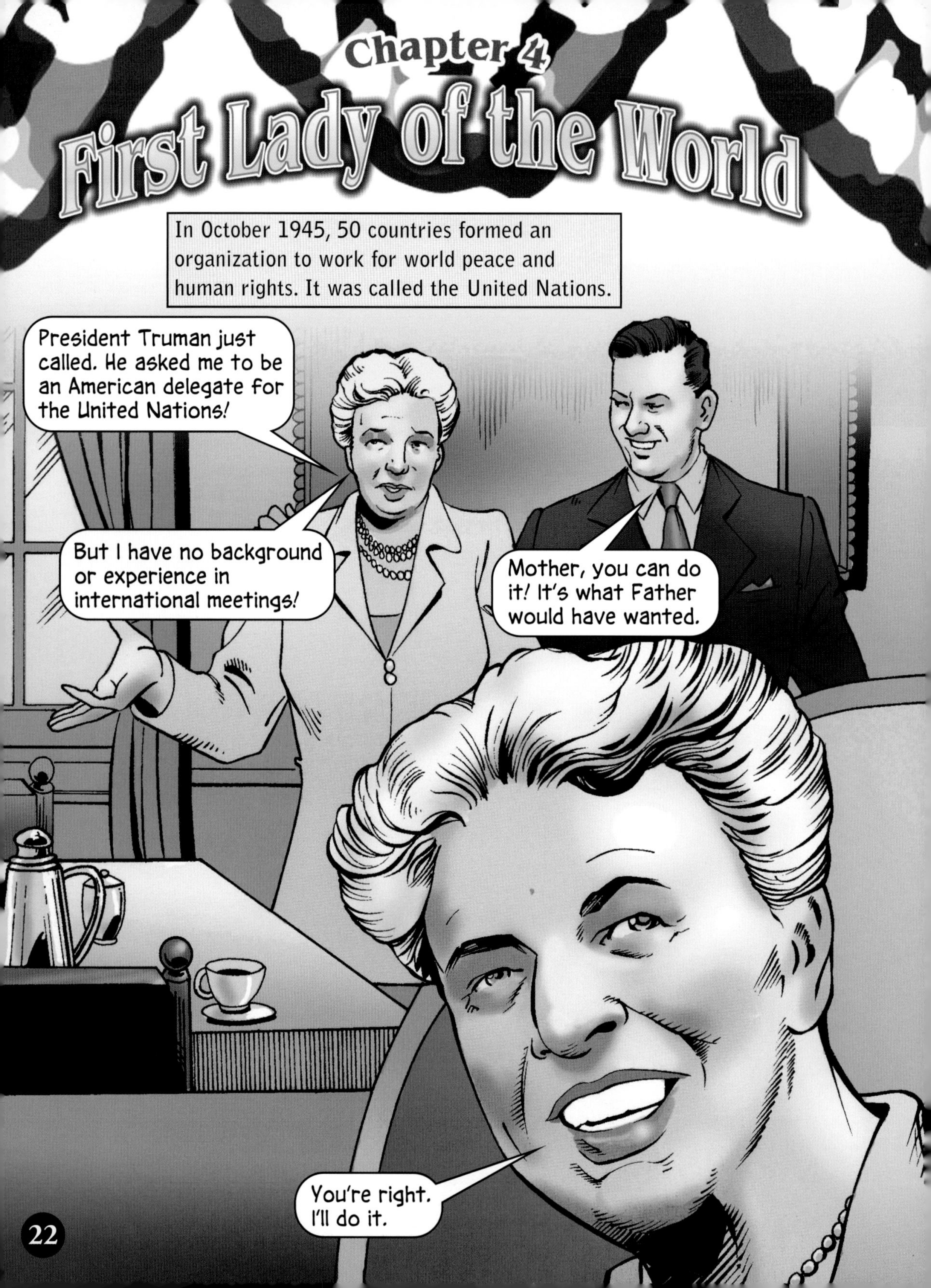
President Truman just called. He asked me to be an American delegate for the United Nations!
But I have no background or experience in international meetings!
Mother, you can do it! It's what Father would have wanted.
You're right. I'll do it.

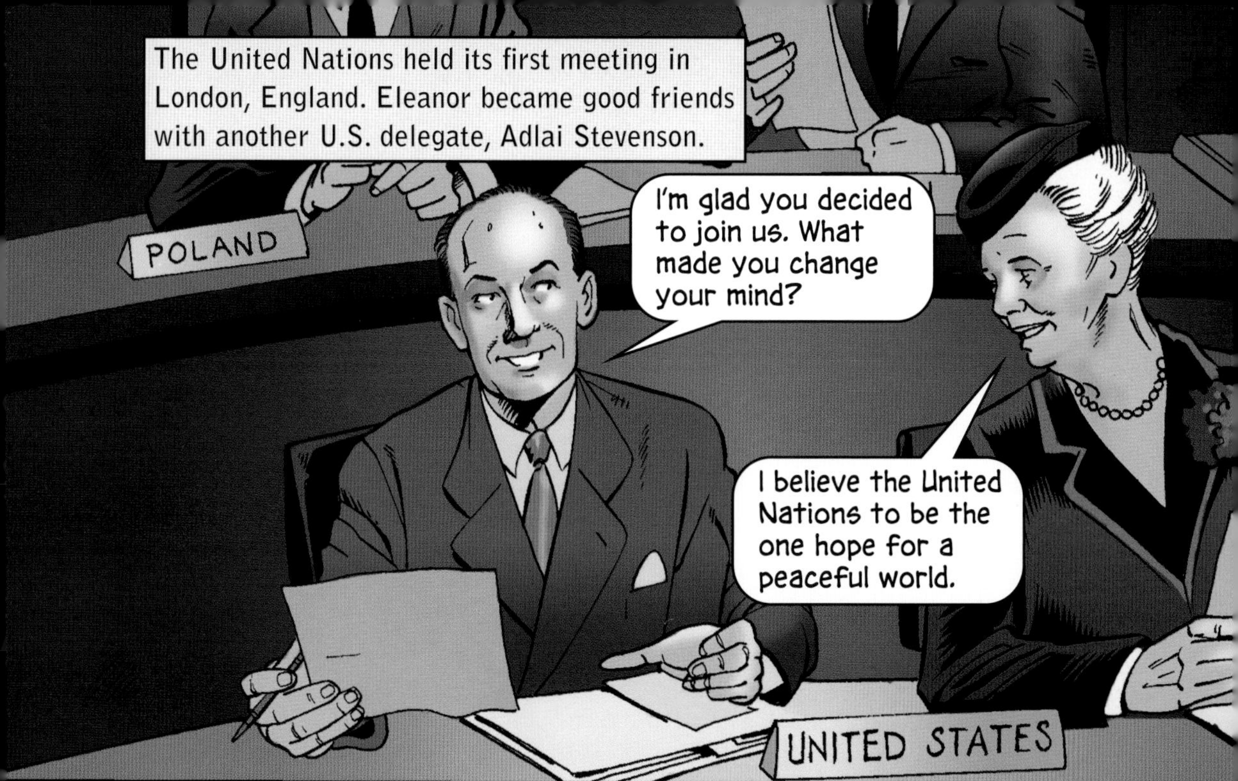
The United Nations held its first meeting in London, England. Eleanor became good friends with another U.S. delegate, Adlai Stevenson.
POLAND
I'm glad you decided to join us. What made you change your mind?
I believe the United Nations to be the one hope for a peaceful world.
UNITED STATES

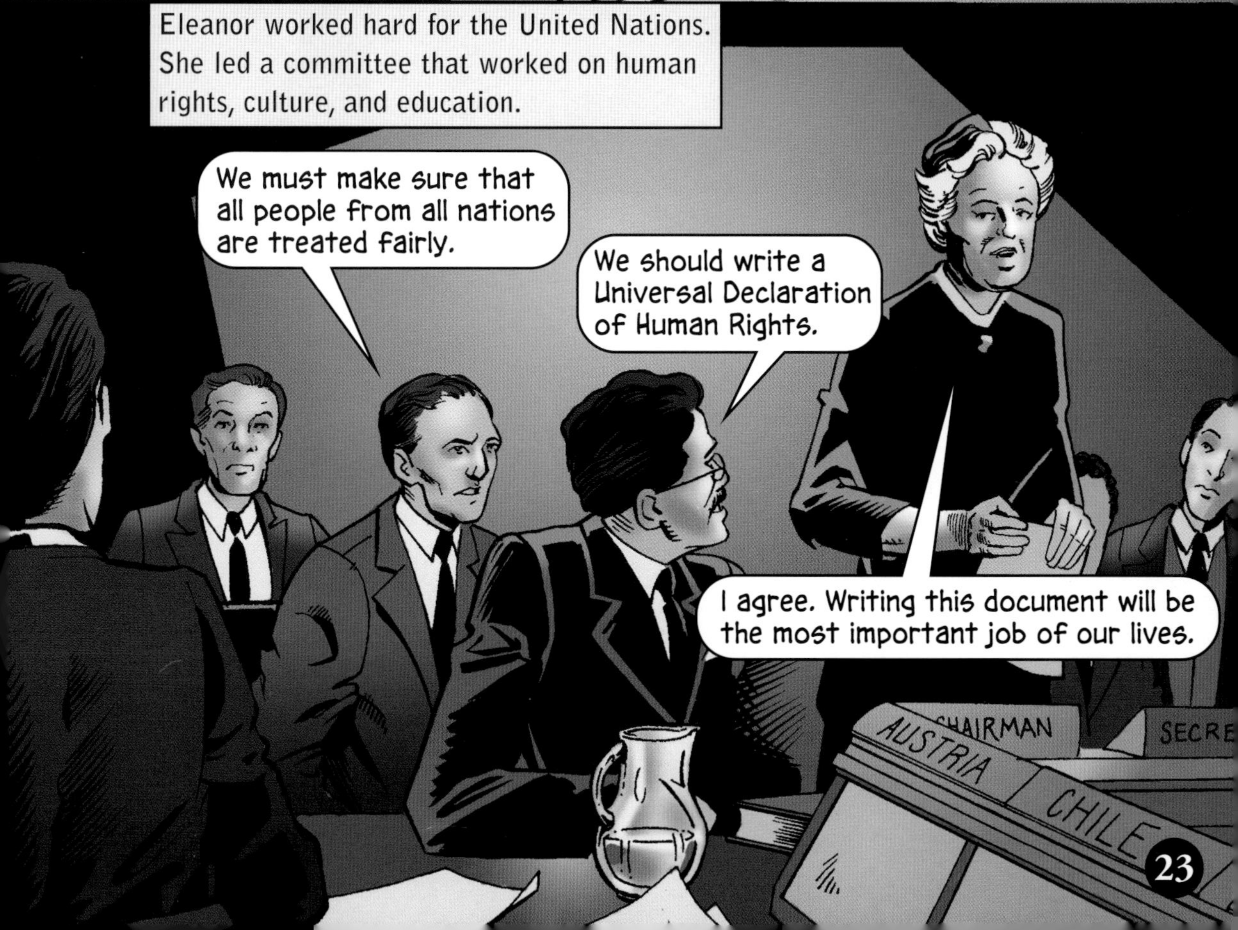
Eleanor worked hard for the United Nations. She led a committee that worked on human rights, culture, and education.
We must make sure that all people from all nations are treated fairly.
We should write a Universal Declaration of Human Rights.
I agree. Writing this document will be the most important job of our lives.
AUSTRIA
CHILE

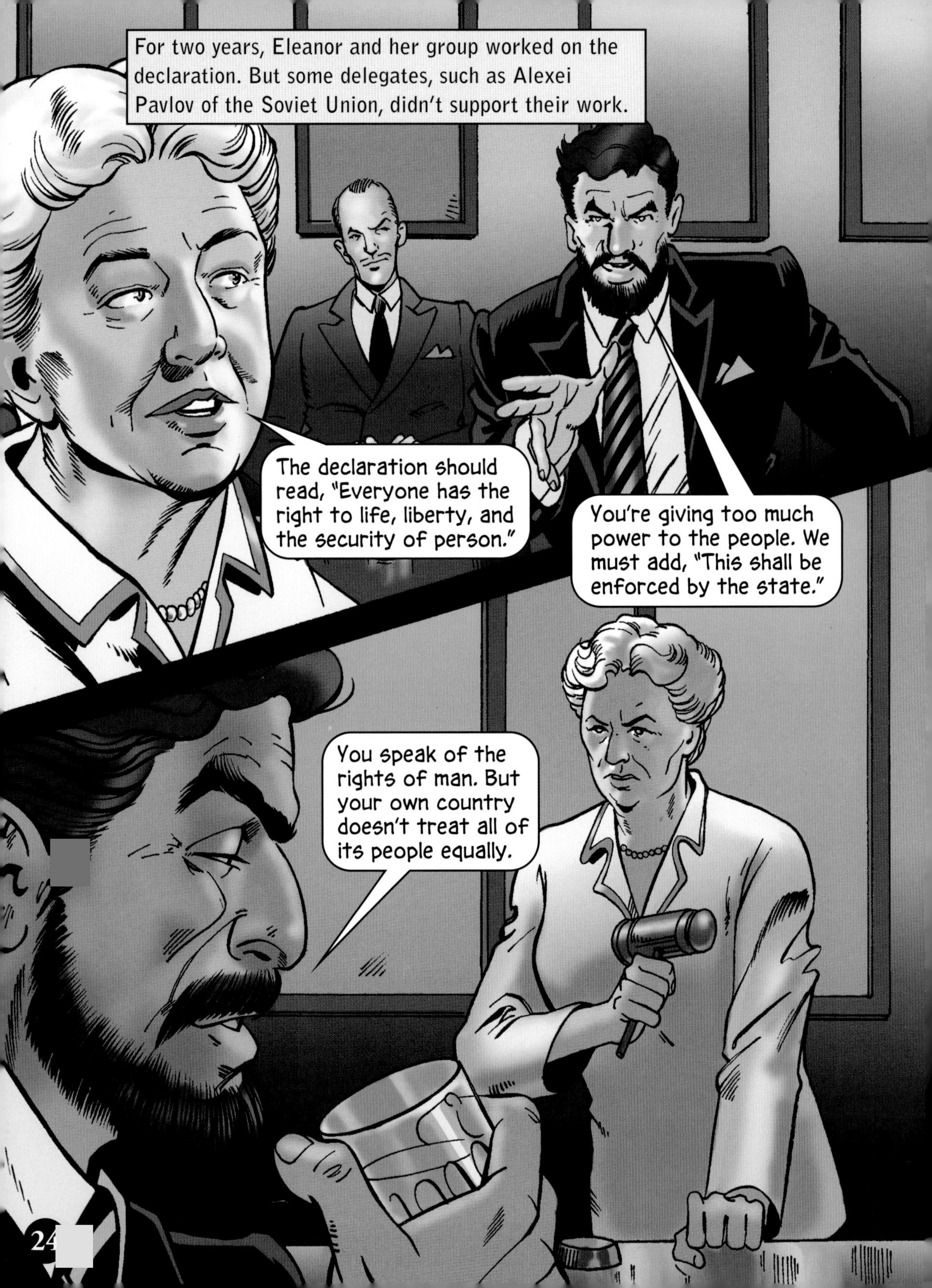
For two years, Eleanor and her group worked on the declaration. But some delegates, such as Alexei Pavlov of the Soviet Union, didn't support their work.
The declaration should read, "Everyone has the right to life, liberty, and the security of person."
You're giving too much power to the people. We must add, "This shall be enforced by the state."
You speak of the rights of man. But your own country doesn't treat all of its people equally.

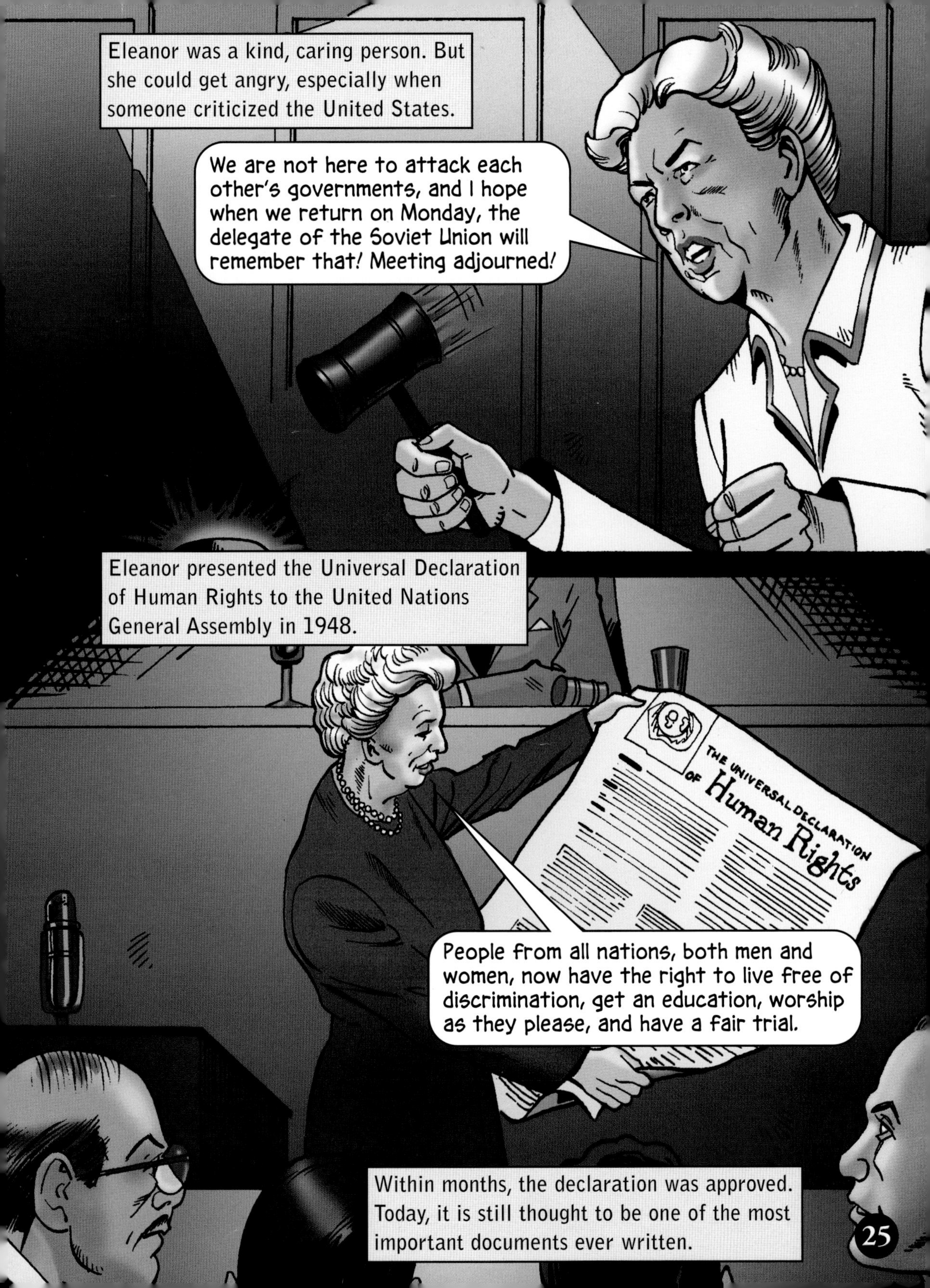
Eleanor was a kind, caring person. But she could get angry, especially when someone criticized the United States.
We are not here to attack each other's governments, and I hope when we return on Monday, the delegate of the Soviet Union will remember that! Meeting adjourned!
Eleanor presented the Universal Declaration of Human Rights to the United Nations General Assembly in 1948.
THE UNIVERSAL DECLARATION OF Human Rights
People from all nations, both men and women, now have the right to live free of discrimination, get an education, worship as they please, and have a fair trial.
Within months, the declaration was approved. Today, it is still thought to be one of the most important documents ever written.

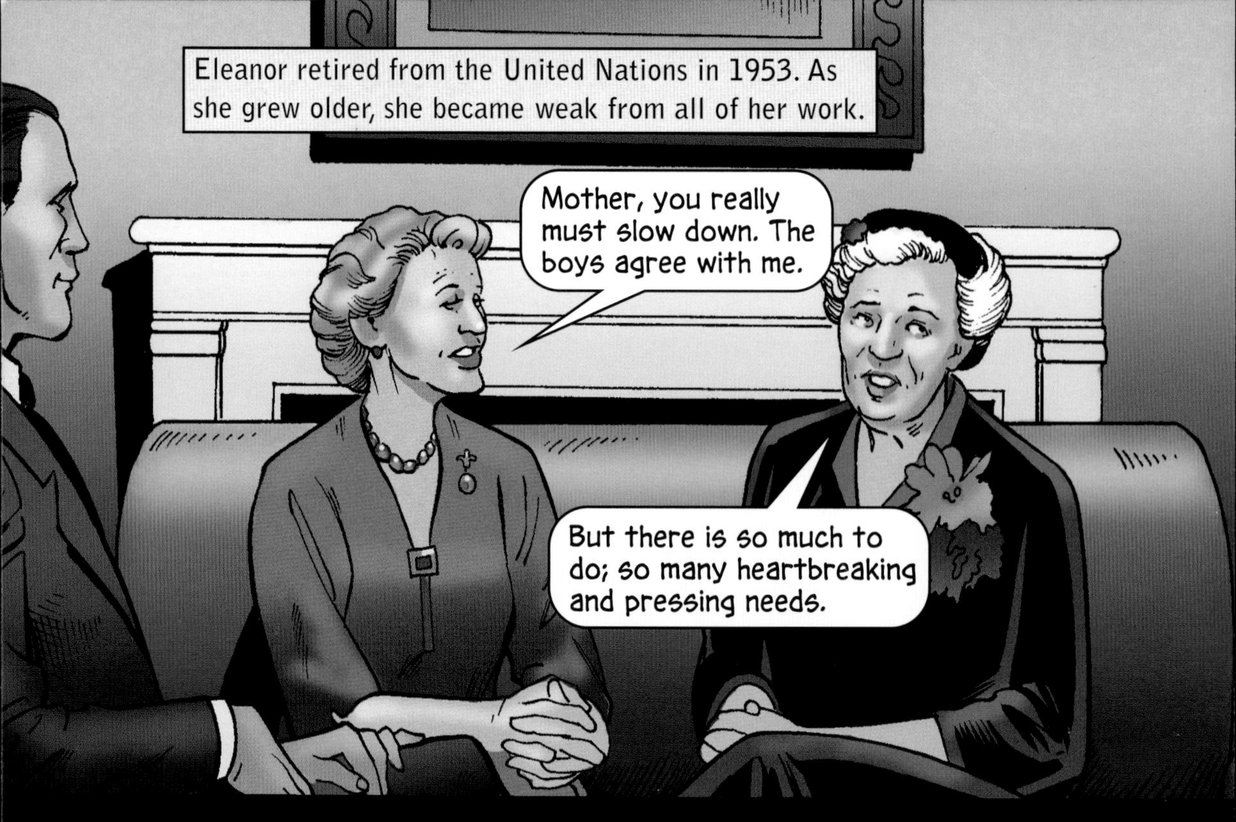
Eleanor retired from the United Nations in 1953. As she grew older, she became weak from all of her work.
Mother, you really must slow down. The boys agree with me.
But there is so much to do; so many heartbreaking and pressing needs.

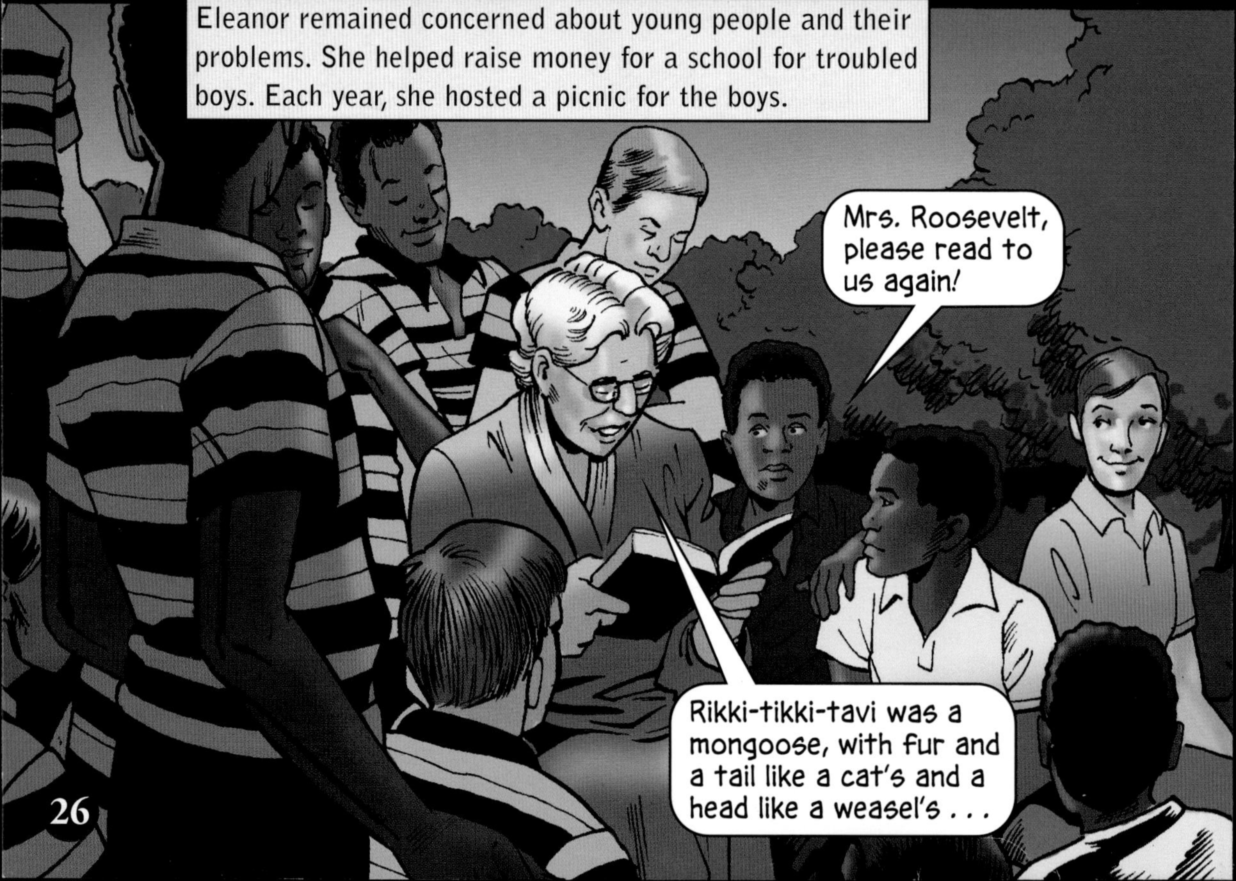
Eleanor remained concerned about young people and their problems. She helped raise money for a school for troubled boys. Each year, she hosted a picnic for the boys.
Mrs. Roosevelt, please read to us again!
Rikki-tikki-tavi was a mongoose, with fur and a tail like a cat's and a head like a weasel's . . .

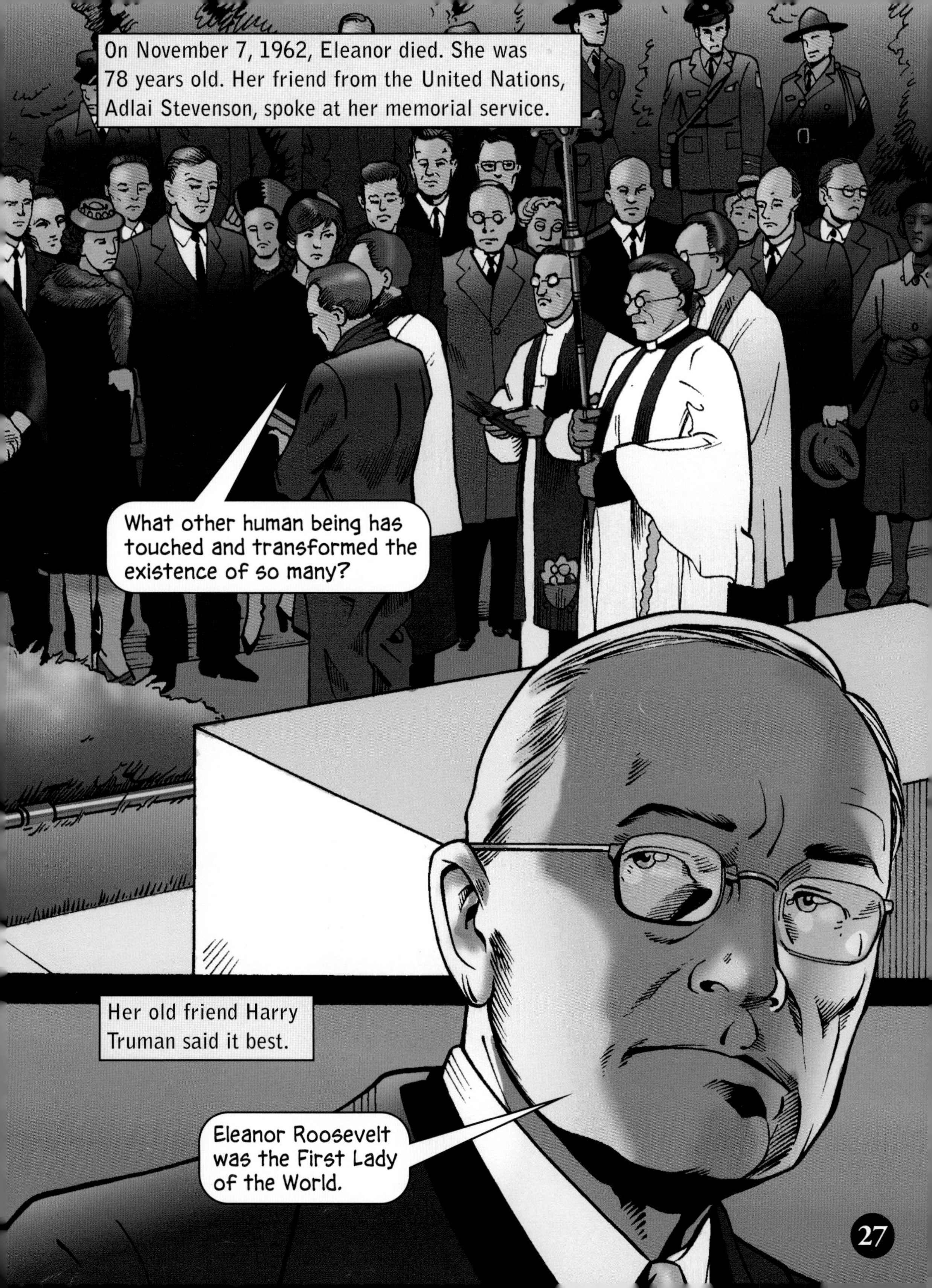

On November 7, 1962, Eleanor died. She was 78 years old. Her friend from the United Nations, Adlai Stevenson, spoke at her memorial service.
What other human being has touched and transformed the existence of so many?
Her old friend Harry Truman said it best.
Eleanor Roosevelt was the First Lady of the World.

More about
ELEANOR ROOSEVELT

- Eleanor was born October 11, 1884, in New York City. Her full name was Anna Eleanor Roosevelt.

- Eleanor's uncle Theodore Roosevelt was the 26th President. He served from 1901 to 1909.

- In the late 1920s, Eleanor helped run the Todhunter School, a private high school for girls in New York City. Eleanor taught classes at the school and also served as its principal for a time.

- Before Eleanor became first lady, most presidents' wives were not a part of politics. But Eleanor changed that. She was the first to fly in a plane, to have a government job, to meet with Congress, to be paid for speaking in public, and to talk on the radio. Eleanor was also the first president's wife to write a daily newspaper column, *My Day*.

- To help women get better jobs, Eleanor sometimes held press conferences where only women were invited. Newspapers had to hire women reporters if they wanted to get the story.

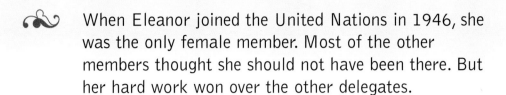 When Eleanor joined the United Nations in 1946, she was the only female member. Most of the other members thought she should not have been there. But her hard work won over the other delegates.

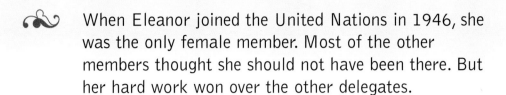 In February 1962, President John F. Kennedy named Eleanor to the President's Commission on the Status of Women. She served on the committee until her death from tuberculosis November 7, 1962.

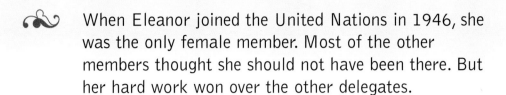 Val-Kill, Eleanor's home in Hyde Park, New York, is the only National Historic Site dedicated to a first lady. Visitors can see Eleanor's cottage, her gardens, and her yard.

GLOSSARY

committee (kuh-MIT-ee)—a group of people who meet to solve a problem or do certain tasks

delegate (DEL-uh-guht)—a person who is sent to represent a group or an organization

governor (GUHV-urn-or)—the leader of a state's executive branch of government

polio (POH-lee-oh)—a disease that attacks the nerves, spinal cord, and brain

tuberculosis (tuh-bur-kyuh-LOH-siss)—a serious and contagious lung disease caused by bacteria

INTERNET SITES

FactHound offers a safe, fun way to find Internet sites related to this book. All of the sites on FactHound have been researched by our staff.

Here's how:

1. Visit *www.facthound.com*
2. Type in this special code **0736849696** for age-appropriate sites. Or enter a search word related to this book for a more general search.
3. Click on the **Fetch It** button.

FactHound will fetch the best sites for you!

READ MORE

Rosenberg, Pam. *Eleanor Roosevelt: First Lady, Humanitarian, and World Citizen.* Our People. Chanhassen, Minn.: Child's World, 2004.

Stone, Amy. *Eleanor Roosevelt.* Raintree Biographies. Austin, Texas: Raintree Steck-Vaughn, 2003.

Winget, Mary. *Eleanor Roosevelt.* History Maker Bios. Minneapolis: Lerner, 2003.

Winner, David. *Eleanor Roosevelt: First Lady of the World.* World Peacemakers. San Diego: Blackbirch Press, 2004.

BIBLIOGRAPHY

Eleanor Roosevelt Center at Val-Kill
http://www.ervk.org

Franklin and Eleanor Roosevelt Institute
http://www.feri.org.

Hareven, Tamara K. *Eleanor Roosevelt: An American Conscience.* Chicago: Quadrangle Books, 1968.

Lash, Joseph P. *Eleanor and Franklin: The Story of Their Relationship, Based on Eleanor Roosevelt's Private Papers.* New York: Norton, 1971.

Roosevelt, Eleanor. *The Autobiography of Eleanor Roosevelt.* New York: Harper & Brothers, 1961.

INDEX